The Love Joy Peace

WORKBOOK

D1472634

The Love Joy Peace

WORKBOOK

A Couple's Bible Study

KIM BOWEN, LPC

ROCKRIDGE PRESS

Interior and Cover Designer: Peatra Jariya
Art Producer: Sue Smith
Editor: Lauren O'Neal
Production Editor: Matthew Burnett
Production Manager: Riley Hoffman
Illustrations: © iStock and © Shutterstock.

ISBN: Print 978-1-64152-844-3 I eBook 978-1-64152-845-0

FOR JOHN.

♡

MY ROMANCE

DOESN'T NEED A THING BUT YOU.

CONTENTS

⊳—♡→

viii	Introduction	
x	How To Use This Book	
1	CHAPTER 1:	Communication
23	CHAPTER 2:	Connection
43	CHAPTER 3:	Conflict
69	CHAPTER 4:	Partnership
85	CHAPTER 5:	Family
97	CHAPTER 6:	Money
113	CHAPTER 7:	Sex
131	CHAPTER 8:	Commitment
150	Resources	
152	References	
153	Index	

INTRODUCTION

*"But the fruit of the Spirit is love,
joy, peace, forbearance, kindness,
goodness, faithfulness, gentleness
and self-control."*

—GALATIANS 5:22–23

Our Father loves us unconditionally, and He calls us to love each other unconditionally, too, even when it's difficult to do. The command is to love both our friends and our enemies. You'd think it would be easier to love our spouses than anyone else, right? Apparently not. According to divorce statistics released by the Barna Group, even among believers, divorce rates hover at about 33 percent.

My husband and I easily could have contributed to that figure. Many years ago, I truly wanted out of my marriage. I knew how my husband needed to change, but I had little insight into my own areas of emotional immaturity. But God used the difficulties in my marriage to refine and mature me. It was painful, but God never left me alone the whole time I was in the fire.

After that experience, and as a professional marriage therapist, I've given a lot of thought to why couples divorce. Taking mental illness, addiction, or abuse out of the equation, I think it boils down to three basic causes:

1. **Poor relationship skills.** Negotiating differences is a skill that has to be learned and practiced. In this workbook, I will define key relationship skills and give you exercises that will help you improve them.
2. **Emotional immaturity.** Learning to regulate your emotions and stop reacting to stress or conflict in negative ways means choosing to grow up emotionally. Fortunately, it's never too late to "grow ourselves up," and this workbook is a great way to start.
3. **Unrealistic expectations.** Too often, I hear clients say, "I *love* my spouse but I'm not *in love* with him or her" or "Love shouldn't be this hard." But love is much more than a feeling—it is a choice. In Zechariah 13:9, God declares He'll put His people "into the fire, and refine them as one refines silver, and test them as gold is tested" (ESV). The struggles that arise in marriages are an effective way to refine us to look more like Christ, if we don't walk away when things get tough.

God uses challenging situations to grow us emotionally so that we can be more like Him. If your marriage is in a difficult season, I encourage you to view it as an opportunity to learn something about yourself and ask God if there is some area of your life He wants to develop. I invite you to approach this workbook and the exercises as a way to gain insight into yourself and the marriage you and your spouse are building. My prayer for you is that God will use the lessons here to bless your covenant. I am praying for your love, joy, and peace!

HOW TO USE THIS BOOK

This workbook is intended to be educational, inspirational, and experiential. It is a Bible study that welcomes both you and your spouse to spend time in the Word of God together, but it is also filled with information and exercises I use in my marriage-counseling practice to help couples heal and deepen their connection. It's a road map to a marriage full of love, joy, and peace—the way it should be.

WHAT'S IN THIS BOOK?

This book consists of eight chapters; each uses scripture and workbook exercises to cover a specific topic. Take your time with each one. The exercises will be more meaningful if you spend time reflecting, praying individually, and discussing the content with your partner. I recommend doing one or two exercises per day and spending one or two weeks on each chapter. You'll benefit most if you and your spouse keep the same pace. I recommend reading a section together and finding a quiet space alone to complete the exercises in that section individually. Once both of you have done an exercise, compare and talk about your answers before moving on to the next section. You don't have to read the chapters in order, but I do recommend reading the first three chapters first, as they'll give you some foundational skills that will help you get the most from the rest of the book.

WHO CAN USE THIS BOOK?

This book is for married couples who want to grow closer to God and to each other, whether you're newlyweds or have been married for decades (or even if you're engaged). It's designed for two spouses to work on together, but if your spouse doesn't want to participate, you can still benefit from working through it on your own. Bonus: The skills, tools, and biblical principles you'll learn here will benefit *all* your relationships.

WHAT MATERIALS DO I NEED?

First and foremost, you'll need a Bible. You'll also need a pen or pencil and paper so that both you and your spouse can make notes and do exercises independently. (A cup of hot tea or coffee can be a nice companion, as well!) Note that instead of including the text of Bible verses, I've included lines for you to write the verses out. Of course, you can choose to simply read them silently or aloud from your Bible, but I find rewriting them helps me concentrate on what they're really saying (and allows you to use your favorite translation).

A NOTE ON ABUSE

Unfortunately, I know that some of my readers will be in marriages that contain emotional or physical abuse. God does not intend for you to live in that situation. For more information and help, please consult the Resources section (page 150).

WORDS OF ENCOURAGEMENT

I encourage you to approach this study with the understanding that all marriages have room for growth and improvement, but change is hard and takes time. Be patient with yourselves and with each other. Couples can easily get discouraged when they've learned new skills but find themselves slipping back into old patterns. Slipping back is part of the process of change! You may feel you aren't making progress, but finding yourself in a familiar painful cycle doesn't mean you aren't changing. Marriage can be really hard at times, but God has a plan for you, and you are not alone.

COMMUNICATION

Communication is the lifeblood of any relationship, and we're always communicating—whether we realize it or not—with our words, tone, body language, and actions. When you make the effort to communicate, with God or with your spouse, you're showing that you value the relationship. Don't be hard on yourselves if you struggle here. Like any skill, communication requires education and practice. But your efforts will be rewarded with greater love, joy, and peace rather than the pain and destruction I see when couples don't learn to communicate well. If you grasp the importance of this skill and dedicate yourselves to using it consistently, there is nothing you and your spouse can't work through together.

▷—♡—→

COMMUNICATING WITH GOD

Good communication, with God or anyone else, requires both talking and listening. God longs to communicate with you, and He has provided ways for you to both talk and listen to Him through His Word, the Holy Spirit, and prayer. When you're in conversation with God, you develop a deeper relationship with your Creator, and as in any relationship, the more time you spend together, the more intimacy and connection you will have—and the better you'll understand how intimacy and connection should work in your marriage.

PRAY CONTINUALLY

Write out 1 Thessalonians 5:16–18.

_____

_____

_____

Scripture tells us to pray without ceasing, which might sound impossible—if you view prayer only as a formal discourse with a beginning and an end. My husband and I have many brief playful or encouraging conversations during the day; I often speak to the Lord the same way, even if it's only one or two sentences as I go about my day. I send up a "thank you" when the weather is nice or ask Him for guidance before a client walks into my office. It's great to go somewhere private and spend long moments in prayer and petition, but if that's the only way you communicate with God, you might find it too overwhelming to do on a daily basis. Life is busy, and we get distracted by so many things. But when you have an ongoing, continual abiding presence with God, you will feel He is always within reach.

If you're stuck in a rut with your prayer life, consider some of the following methods of communicating with God:

Prayer journaling. Write your prayer like you're writing God a letter.

Praying scripture. Select a Bible verse that's meaningful to you (Psalms is a good place to start), and speak it aloud to God.

Walking prayer. Take a walk outside. Spend time noticing God's creation and finding beauty in His work. Express your gratitude for what you see aloud or silently.

Intercessory prayer. Make a list of people in your life who are important to you. Beside each name, write a specific prayer request you have for that person.

Lectio divina. (My personal favorite!) This Latin phrase means "divine reading." It is an ancient tradition, and it has separate steps: scripture reading, meditation, prayer, and contemplation. When I practice *lectio divina*, I ask God to open my heart and show me what He wants me to know through the Bible.

EXERCISE: THE PROMISE OF PRAYER

Write out each of the following scriptures and discuss with each other the ways you'll benefit from praying. When has God fulfilled His promise to answer your prayers, even if it was in an unexpected way?

Matthew 21:22

1 John 5:14-15

2 Chronicles 7:14

_____

_____

_____

_____

Write 2 Timothy 3:16.

_____

_____

_____

We speak to God through prayer, and God speaks to us through His Word. We cannot know the will of God unless we spend time listening to what He tells us. Scripture allows us to learn more about who God is, how He loves us, and how we need to act. His Word challenges us to grow and mature as His followers and is our road map for living. Hebrews 4:12 says that "the word of God is living and active" (ESV). To me, that means God speaks to me through His Word based on what I need to hear at any given point in my life. A single verse can speak truth to you in a way that feels as if it were written just for you at that very time and place. You may read the same verse another time and get an equally relevant but very different message. Only a living and active book could do that.

With your spouse, choose a verse or passage of scripture, then spend some time reading and meditating on the words separately. Ask God to speak to you through His Word. Write down any observations or what you think God might be telling you. The Lord's Prayer (Matthew 6:5–13) is a good place to start.

_____

_____

_____

_____

TALKING WITH GOD TOGETHER

Write out Acts 1:13–14.

_____

_____

_____

_____

The only thing more beneficial than praying is praying with other believers. God hears our prayers when we're alone or in a group, but when we're vulnerable with each other about our worries, fears, or struggles, we can "carry each other's burdens" (Galatians 6:2).

I'll never forget the first time my husband and I prayed together. John is a man of few words, and if I'm not careful, I can easily end up doing all the talking. Hearing him pray was a good opportunity for me to just listen and let him speak his thoughts aloud. This wasn't a prayer he would share in front of other people. I listened as he asked God to give him wisdom and relieve his stress at work—which was surprising because he hadn't mentioned this stress to me. I marveled at the depth of the love he expressed for his family, and I felt safer and more cherished as he prayed protection over us.

I often tell clients that intimacy is so much more than sex. Intimacy is "into me you see." I'm not sure anything else we've done has made me feel more intimate with John than praying together. Praying as a couple can seem awkward or embarrassing at first. Some couples even feel it's "too much" intimacy. But I encourage you to try it, even if it feels difficult—*especially* if it feels difficult—because that kind of vulnerability is the glue that holds marriages together. If one or both of you is hesitant, start small with a safe subject like your jobs or your kids. Pray authentically in your own voice without worrying about how "deep" or "spiritual" you sound. God knows your heart; just talk to Him like He's sitting right there with you.

EXERCISE: PRAYING AS A COUPLE

Do you have concerns about praying with your spouse? If so, what are they?

Is there anything your spouse can say or do that would make it easier for you to pray together?

Whether you decide to pray together or separately, it is wise to pray *for* each other. Write down three concerns or requests you'd like your spouse to bring to God in prayer on your behalf.

Schedule a time to pray together that works for both of you, and write it on the following line. Set a reminder on your phone to alert you when it's time to pray together each week.

_____

COMMUNICATING AS A COUPLE

Write out James 1:19.

_____

_____

_____

_____

One of the most common statements made in a couple's first therapy session is: "We can't communicate." What that really means is that they don't yet understand the three basic components of healthy, effective communication:

1. The message sent.
2. The message received.
3. The message intended.

The speaker has control over the way the message is delivered, and the listener has control over how the message is received. It takes both of them to work together, through dialogue, to understand the intent. The intent is often the piece of the puzzle that is lost in translation. To communicate well as a couple, you both must get clarity on all three of these areas.

When you're the one sending the message, you'll be a more effective speaker if you remember that words have power: "The soothing tongue is a tree of life, but a perverse tongue crushes the spirit" (Proverbs 15:4). If you speak with anger, criticism, or cruelty, you have almost certainly derailed communication from the start. Even if your words are perfectly stated, your partner is receiving them through the filter of his or her current frame of mind and past experience. Your body language and tone also affect how your words are received. Don't assume words are enough. Check in with your partner to see if the message they're receiving aligns with the message you're trying to send. Too often, senders get frustrated when they feel misunderstood and either stop talking or start yelling. Instead, ask questions.

When you're the one receiving the message, it helps to remember that being in the listener role can be the hardest part of communication because it requires patience and emotional self-regulation, especially if you don't like what you're hearing. But the Bible says that "to answer before listening... is folly and shame" (Proverbs 18:13). When you respond with denial, defensiveness, or anger, you create a rupture in the relationship that encourages your spouse to stay quiet or, worse, lie to you. Train yourself not only to listen with humility and grace but also to ask questions before you react. Make sure you understand the message your partner is *intending*, which may not align well with his or her words or tone.

Identify a topic that is slightly uncomfortable to discuss, such as you or your partner not picking up dirty clothes from the floor. Stand facing each other, about six feet apart. Take turns as speaker and listener. The speaker's goal is to get his or her message across using words, tone, facial expressions, and body language. The listener should step closer only when he or she feels the speaker is being respectful or endearing. The listener should take a step backward if the speaker is communicating in a way that creates distance, such as using critical words, a harsh tone, or defensive posture. If the listener is able to get close enough to the speaker, hug each other for a job well done!

HURTFUL HABITS

Write out Psalm 141:3.

_____

_____

The Bible warns us to keep our tongues in check because we can do so much harm with our words. It's normal to feel angry, but be careful about what you say. I've seen so many couples be plain mean to each other, expressing contempt with snarky comments, insults, constant criticism, and eye-rolling. This atmosphere creates hurtful habits that are hard to break. We all have bad days where we say something hurtful to our spouses, but when this behavior is prevalent, we cross the line into verbal and emotional abuse.

If you treat your spouse with disrespect or cruelty, it says more about you and your limitations than about your spouse's flaws. We often attack what we cannot change in our spouses instead of changing how we respond to them. This kind of attack rarely alters their behavior, and when it does, it comes at the cost of connection, trust, safety, and love. Focusing on your spouse keeps you stuck in unhealthy cycles of blame and resentment. Focusing on how you respond to your spouse is the quickest way to change a negative pattern.

Think of a time when you were critical or cruel to your spouse. You were probably feeling angry or frustrated. Write down the details of the event and what you said or did in response.

_____

_____

_____

_____

_____

When you said and did those things, what were you hoping your spouse would think, feel, and do?

1. Think?

_____

_____

2. Feel?

_____

_____

3. Do?

_____

_____

_____

Looking back, do you think your words or actions got the desired response?

Yes or No (circle your answer)

Now imagine being your spouse at the moment you were being unkind.

What do you imagine your spouse thought, felt, and did?

1. Thought?

_____

_____

_____

2. Felt?

_____

_____

_____

3. Did?

_____

_____

_____

Here are some common forms of harmful communication styles in marriages.

Criticism. Finding something wrong or frequently pointing out what "should" have been done differently.

Speaking in absolutes. "You always say this," "You never do that."

Mockery or sarcasm. Belittling your spouse with words or actions that humiliate or shame him or her.

Lying. Being untruthful to avoid a confrontation or consequence.

Blame and defensiveness. Not taking ownership for your part or turning things back on your spouse.

Neglect. Spending too much time on devices, at work, or with friends; unilaterally withholding sex.

Betraying confidence. Speaking negatively about your spouse to others or sharing intimate details about your spouse that you know you shouldn't.

Raging. Screaming, yelling, throwing a tantrum, or slamming doors.

Pouting. Being silent, grumpy, or aloof to show displeasure.

Smothering or clinging. Not allowing your partner to have personal space; feeling rejected when your partner wants time alone or with friends.

Threats. Threats to divorce, take the kids or money away, or use violence as a way to manipulate or control your spouse.

Physical violence. Shoving, hitting, slapping, throwing things at each other, or holding someone against his or her will. If you're in a physically violent relationship, please consult the Resources section (page 150) for information and help.

It's time for a gut check. How often have you used the following hurtful habits in the past 30 days?

HABIT	NOT AT ALL	OCCASIONALLY	SOMEWHAT OFTEN	VERY OFTEN
Criticism				
Speaking in absolutes				
Mockery or sarcasm				
Lying				
Blame or defensiveness				
Neglect				
Betraying confidence				
Raging				
Pouting				
Smothering or clinging				
Threats				
Physical violence				

CASE STUDY: DAN AND CARMEN

Dan and Carmen came to see me because they hadn't been happy in their marriage for a long time. I see a lot of fighting couples in my office, but they took things to a new level. Dan told Carmen he wasn't attracted to her anymore because she was fat, but he got angry if she didn't want sex when he initiated. Carmen regularly belittled Dan, telling him he was stupid and needed to "be a man." Despite these bad habits, they had the one thing that makes change possible no matter how bad things have become: motivation! Both were tired of living in a war zone and were ready to try something new. They learned new ways to express frustration and disappointment without hurting each other and how to make quick repair when things did go badly. Their marriage needed a lot of work, but they both were surprised at how much happier they became once they simply started being nicer to each other. Good marriages require good manners. This couple was so used to ugly verbal sparring that they forgot how peaceful it could be to just treat each other with common civility. They took divorce off the table, and they continue to heal and grow closer—and it all started with just treating each other with respect.

No matter how many of these you or your spouse checked, your marriage can see great improvement if you become aware of bad habits; hold yourself accountable for them; and replace them with new, more loving ones.

HEALTHY HABITS

Write down the following verses and consider what God says about the power of our words.

Proverbs 16:24

Proverbs 15:1

Proverbs 11:17

I can't think of anything more powerful and healing in any relationship than simply being kind to each other. If you keep your emotions regulated, you can talk about your hurt or anger in a way that lets your spouse hear it and respond. Just as angry words can wound, kind words can heal.

What does healthy communication look like? Here are some good habits to develop:

Listen and be curious. Ask questions and be open to discovering why your partner has a different perspective.

Don't assume what your spouse says is about *you*. Often, it's about your spouse and what's going on in his or her head.

State your thoughts or feelings without blame. Avoid "you" statements ("You never clean up after yourself"). Instead, use "I" statements ("I get frustrated when the house is a mess, and I'd love your help keeping it clean").

Give up wanting to be right. If one of you wins, you both lose.

Use appropriate humor when possible. Humor cuts the tension and keeps things calm, as long as it isn't mean-spirited or at your spouse's expense.

Don't make assumptions. Tell your spouse how you're interpreting what he or she says, and check in with your spouse to be sure it's accurate. I can assure you that assumptions are wrong far more often than they're right. I teach my clients to say, "What I make up about what you just said is…." This one phrase can defuse many bombs.

When your spouse hurts your feelings, let him or her know how you feel and how he or she can make repair. Here is one example: "When you didn't invite me to dinner with your friends, I felt unwanted and left out. I'd like you to tell me you understand how I could feel that way and reassure me this doesn't have anything to do with me—you just want time alone with your friends."

When you blow it, own it quickly. We all mess up, especially if we're trying to learn new habits. When you fall back into old patterns, apologize as soon as you calm down. Don't make excuses. Ask your spouse what you could do or say to make him or her feel better.

Be honest. Trust is lost by the bucket and gained by the teaspoon. Honesty is more than not lying; it's being open and willing to share, even if it causes you anxiety or creates tension.

Share appreciations. Remember that it takes ten positive comments to balance one negative remark.

Keep calm. Even if your spouse is losing it, learn to regulate yourself emotionally. If you can't, take a time-out and come back to the topic when you're both calm.

Make a list of the positive ways your spouse contributes to the marriage. Then share your list with your spouse and express appreciation.

ACTIONS AND WORDS

Write out 1 John 3:18.

In this verse, we're told to love with our words *and* our actions. I often see people whose words and actions do not align. They tell me they love their spouses, but their actions show me something else. When words and actions don't align, I always believe the actions.

In his book *The Five Love Languages*, Gary Chapman describes the five main ways people communicate love with actions: giving gifts, spending quality time, speaking words of affirmation, performing acts of service, and expressing love by physical touch. We tend to give love in the way we want to receive it, but if our spouse's love language is different from ours, they might miss the loving message we're trying to send.

Years ago, I'd try to show my husband I was thinking of him by bringing home shirts I thought he'd like when I went shopping. I still remember the day he casually said he prefers picking out his own clothes. I was pouring out my love with every shirt I bought him, but his love language is acts of service; when I set the trash cans on the curb, he feels all fuzzy and warm, but buying him clothes does nothing for him. Go figure!

EXERCISE: YOUR LOVE LANGUAGES

Which of the five love languages do you most identify with? If you're not sure, you can take a short, free quiz at 5lovelanguages.com. Write your love language, or top two languages, here:

_____

_____

_____

_____

Write down three to five things you'd like your spouse to consider doing for you that would help him or her speak in your love language.

_____

_____

_____

_____

LISTENING WITH YOUR WHOLE FACE

Have you ever been at a social gathering when someone asked you how you were doing, but a lack of eye contact told you he or she didn't really care about your answer? Or have you told someone you were "fine" when your body language clearly showed you weren't? We can verbally say the right thing, but if our nonverbal communication is off, the message will fall flat.

Once, when I was talking to my husband, he was nodding his head and saying "uh-huh" in all the right places, but I could tell he wasn't listening. When I went silent and he asked me what was wrong, I said I was done talking until he could "listen with his whole face"! We laugh about that now, but sometimes I still remind him to listen to me with his whole face, by making eye contact and showing genuine interest. When his words, actions, and body language are aligned, I feel heard.

Now that many of us spend our days bent over our phone screens, I see increasingly more unhappy couples who feel they're being neglected for their spouses' screen time. Try listening to your spouse with your whole face for one week, and see what happens!

Share this list with your spouse. Once you have your spouse's list, pick at least one thing from that list and commit to doing it at least once or twice over the next week. You can make a fun game of this by not telling your spouse which item(s) you chose and letting him or her guess.

REVIEW

Here's a quick review of what we discussed in this chapter:

- God teaches us how to listen and speak to Him and to each other.
- Praying as a couple increases intimacy and lets us see our spouses differently. As I mentioned, intimacy is "into me you see," and it's about revealing our innermost thoughts and feelings without being judged or condemned for them.

- Communication involves three elements: the message sent, the message received, and the message intended.
- Hurtful communication habits, such as criticism, blame, lies, and threats, can destroy marriages and need to be taken seriously. Do not minimize or deny the effects they have on your spouse.
- Healthy communication habits, such as using "I" statements, explaining how you feel, and making quick repair when you mess up, build a foundation of trust and love in your marriage.
- Actions and nonverbal communication speak as loudly as words.

TAKE COURAGE AND DO IT

Here are five actions to take during the next week to foster peaceful and loving communication with your spouse:

1. Pray together as a couple, and pray for each other.
2. Catch your spouse doing something right and praise these efforts. Be a detective looking for ways your spouse has shown up, delivered on a promise, controlled his or her temper, or taken initiative.
3. Share at least one message of appreciation with your spouse each day.
4. Turn off your phones at dinner each night and focus on being together as a couple or family. If this feels awkward, that's a sign that you need to do it.
5. Plan a date night and enjoy time with your spouse. Use that time to do something you both enjoy. Avoid tough conversations or discussing work or kids. Ask your spouse questions like you've just met and want to get to know him or her.

CONNECTION

God's divine plan for creation was always centered around connection—with Him and with each other. People are messy and complicated, and nothing teaches us more about God's love and grace than being in a relationship with our spouses. In my work as a marriage therapist, I see how difficult it is to be in any relationship where there has been pain, rejection, or betrayal. It's natural to want to isolate, withdraw, or retaliate when we're hurting, but authentic connection with God and with our spouses is what brings us joy, peace, and happiness.

CONNECTING WITH GOD

Write out Luke 15:3-4.

_____

_____

_____

I love this example of how God pursues us. He doesn't get tangled up in feelings of hurt or rejection when we turn away. He knows we are going to make mistakes, and yet He loves us and wants a relationship with us. Let's explore how to cultivate that connection with God.

GOD WANTS TO CONNECT WITH YOU

Write out Luke 10:27.

_____

_____

_____

The Greatest Commandment, as Luke 10:27 is often called, tells us how to love and connect with God and with others. That connection has four dimensions: heart, soul, mind, and strength. God wants the whole of us, not just the parts we feel like sharing. This type of connection takes ongoing effort and practice and equips us to fully connect with God and with our spouses.

EXERCISE: THE GREATEST COMMANDMENT

What do you think it means to love God with all your:

Heart (desires, passions, longings)?

_____

_____

_____

_____

Soul (personality, spirituality, immortal self)?

_____

_____

_____

_____

Mind (thoughts, intentions, intellect)?

_____

_____

_____

_____

Strength (physical strength, assets, resources)?

_____

_____

_____

When you feel disconnected from God, which aspect of connection is likely the weakest and why?

_____

_____

_____

What do you think it means to love your spouse with all your:

Heart (desires, passions, longings)?

_____

_____

_____

Soul (personality, spirituality, immortal self)?

Mind (thoughts, intentions, intellect)?

Strength (physical strength, assets, resources)?

When you feel disconnected from your spouse, which aspect of connection is likely the weakest, and why?

Do you notice any parallels in your answers regarding loving God and loving your spouse? Reflect on that below.

CONSTANT CONTACT WITH GOD

Write out Psalm 42:1-2.

CASE STUDY: KEN AND CAROL

Many marriages fail when spouses evaluate the strength of their connection based on emotions alone. Emotions come and go, but if your commitment is to love with your whole heart, soul, strength, and mind, you're choosing to connect even when fickle feelings temporarily wane. A lifelong marriage requires this kind of commitment.

Ken and Carol came to therapy because Carol wanted a trial separation. She believed her marriage was over because she no longer felt she was in love with Ken. But through counseling, Carol realized that her feelings were largely the result of exhaustion. She had a demanding full-time job and was raising seven-year-old triplets while also trying to manage Ken's anxiety by making sure everything was done at home how he wanted it. No wonder she wasn't feeling love for him! Carol stuck with the marriage and with counseling, and decided her commitment mattered more than her feelings. After several months of making changes and exploring her emotions, she noticed, to her surprise, that her feelings for Ken were beginning to return, even though she'd been sure she was done when she first came in to see me. It was a relief for her to discover she could feel love and passion for her husband again. She regained that connection through the kind of commitment God models for us.

When I was a young mother, I moved with my husband and children to a new city and quickly found a church of strong believers. I participated in the women's Bible class and was immediately struck by the people who spoke about having regular "God time" and how much they craved this time to pray and read scripture. One woman had a dedicated "prayer closet," where she spent an hour each morning. I was in a new home in a strange town with two kids under five. I didn't have time to shave my legs, much less find "God time." I wanted to yearn for time with God like David wrote about in Psalm 42:1–2, but the truth was that I yearned for sleep and a clean house more. Adding prayer time to my schedule felt like a burden.

But when I stopped thinking about meeting God as an item on my to-do list and started thinking of it as a spiritual discipline that would bring me closer to

Him, I found ways to connect that suited me in that busy season. The phrase "spiritual discipline" may sound hard and exhausting, but it's just a fancy way of referring to activities that connect us with God, such as prayer, meditation, and fasting. Spending time with God does not have to be a formal affair. You can worship, pray, and meditate without having to set aside large blocks of time. The key is to start practicing small daily rituals, one at a time, to avoid getting overwhelmed. Don't add a new one until the current one is second nature. Give yourself permission to find God in ways that work for your lifestyle. He will meet you in this time.

EXERCISE: DAILY RITUALS FOR CONNECTING WITH GOD

What is one activity you already do each day that would allow you to add in a small window of "God time" without adding an extra task? (This could be something like brushing your teeth, loading the dishwasher, or walking to the bus.)

Choose your daily ritual.

Commit to making one of the following practices part of that daily ritual:

- ❑ Identify five things you're grateful for, and thank God for them.
- ❑ Sing a song of praise, focusing on the words.
- ❑ Pray for your spouse and your marriage.
- ❑ Pray for your kids.
- ❑ Meditate on your blessings with thanksgiving.
- ❑ Ask God to help you in one specific way today.

CONNECTING WITH EACH OTHER

Write out Ecclesiastes 4:9–10.

Over the years, I've witnessed many marriages that felt unfulfilling to one or both partners because they lacked a deep connection. Marriages go through cycles of distance and closeness. You'll have seasons when you feel closer to each other and seasons when you're pulled apart by the demands of jobs, kids, illness, or other stressors. But couples who make the intentional effort to connect with each other are the ones who report the most happiness and satisfaction.

My marriage went through a years-long dry spell in which my husband and I seemed more tired and irritated with each other than close and connected. Eventually, I began fantasizing about divorce. Looking back, it wasn't a single event or rupture that strained us to the breaking point. We'd just fallen out of the habits that kept our marriage strong. Because we were doing okay, it didn't feel that important to put in the energy required to stay connected. This was almost our fatal mistake.

On some level, we all acknowledge that things of value need regular maintenance. We change the oil in our cars and keep our phones charged. But we often neglect our relationships because we take them for granted or let our feelings direct our actions, abandoning our efforts at connection when we get busy, distracted, or irritated. The best way to stay connected with your spouse, whether the two of you are feeling closer or more distant, is the same way we stay connected with God: by setting up routine connection rituals.

Write out Song of Solomon 7:11-12.

Solomon gives us an example of lovers intentionally making time for each other and finding ways to connect. Following is a list of "connectors"—rituals that draw us closer to our spouse. Using them often will help you love your spouse with your heart, soul, mind, and strength.

Spend time alone with each other regularly. This means no kids or other friends. The impact of this connector cannot be overstated, yet the vast majority of couples I see in counseling haven't had "alone time" for a long time. Put this on your calendar, or it won't happen consistently. If you have young kids, schedule a babysitter to come at the same time on the same night of the week so that childcare is always in place.

Have fun! Be playful and flirtatious. Life can get serious quickly, and you have to add some play into your life to balance that out. Play is any activity that is done for no other reason than enjoyment.

Do projects together. Chores don't have to be drudgery if you approach them as an opportunity to spend time together. Try cooking a meal, walking the dog, weeding the garden, or washing the car together. Focus more on enjoying your partner than completing the task perfectly as you work together.

Share some interests. Having your own hobbies apart from your spouse is actually a sign of a healthy marriage, but it's also important to find some interests you share. Shared experiences create closeness and connection, building the foundation for friendship that so many marriages are missing. Some interests that couples share include exercise, travel, gardening, sports, music, the outdoors, and movies.

Touch each other often. Physical intimacy is an important part of connecting as a couple. In my practice, I've discovered that many couples aren't having enough sex. But before they stop having sex, they usually stop having affectionate physical touch. Be intentional about cuddling together when watching TV or reading. Hold hands when you walk.

EXERCISE: IDENTIFYING CONNECTORS

Think back to a time when you and your spouse were dating. What did you do together for fun? What rituals did you regularly engage in that kept you connected? Spend some time thinking and remembering. List as many things as you can.

_____

_____

_____

_____

Is there anything on that list you've stopped doing now that you're married?

_____

_____

_____

_____

Each of you make a list of your favorite hobbies and the activities you do for fun.

Is there anything that made both your lists? If nothing matches, keep brainstorming together until you find at least one activity you both enjoy, then make a date to do it.

Another good way to connect is by going down memory lane together. Look at your wedding photos or video together. Notice who was there. Reminisce about what you were thinking and feeling.

DISCONNECTORS

Write out Deuteronomy 24:5.

As kids come along and careers demand more of our time and energy, it's harder to find time to be together. Be aware of these disconnectors that can sneak into your daily lives. They may not seem like a big deal at first, but they can build up to something bigger over time.

Too much screen time. Between work emails, texts, and social media, we can be distracted and entertained by our phones all day and night. Here are a few tips to help break the habit: Set your phone to stop receiving calls and texts after 9:00 p.m.; silence your phone during dinner; make evenings a "no-work" zone; and, if possible, leave your phone at home when you're out on a date with your spouse.

Inappropriate emotional connections with the opposite sex. Even strong marriages can fall prey to affairs, and social media makes it easy to begin emotional affairs. You may tell yourself it's a harmless friendship, but the minute you start becoming secretive or sharing things that would upset your spouse, you're too far over the line. It is prudent to avoid any private conversations you wouldn't want your spouse to see.

Secrets and dishonesty. Secrets make it hard to maintain "into me you see" intimacy. Secrecy isn't having privacy or a private thought; it's hiding something to avoid a negative consequence. Privacy refers to your own thoughts, beliefs, attitudes, or fantasies, which are yours alone. It's your choice when, how, if, and to whom you'll make them known. (Invading someone's privacy is a disconnector, too. It's not okay to read your partner's email, texts, or journal.)

Lack of empathy. Sometimes we have trouble listening to our partners and expressing empathy without going into problem-solving mode or, worse, lecturing and criticizing. Men in particular tend to try to problem-solve when their wives are upset. They're often shocked when I tell them that this hurts more than it helps. They say, "So what am I supposed to do when she complains about work? Just *listen*?" "Of course not," I tell them. "You have to listen *and* show empathy." That is what makes partners feel seen, heard, and loved—no solutions necessary or even wanted.

Nagging and criticizing your partner. When you complain, your partner feels negatively toward you and often toward themselves. Nagged spouses start to feel there's nothing they can do to please their partners, so they eventually quit trying. Instead of complaining and using words like "never" or "always," try simply asking. Of course, your partner always has the choice to say no, and being in a relationship with someone means learning how to hear no and how to negotiate a win for both parties.

Insisting on being right. You've likely heard the phrase "Do you want to be right or do you want to be married?" Some people die on the hill of needing to be right. Be open to your spouse's viewpoint, even if it's vastly different from yours. Listening and being curious doesn't necessarily mean you agree; it means you're connecting in a healthy way.

List three things your spouse does or says that help you feel more connected to him or her.

_____

_____

_____

List three things your spouse does or says that drives disconnection between you.

_____

_____

_____

Compare your answers and discuss any surprises.

WHAT'S HOLDING YOU BACK?

Write out 1 Peter 3:8.

_____

_____

_____

CREATIVE DATE NIGHT IDEAS

- Take a drive down a road you've never been down before.
- Find a local music venue and see a band or an artist you've never heard.
- Get season tickets for your favorite sports team or for the theater, opera, or symphony.
- Read the Bible together.
- Go to a flea market or an antique show.
- Take a weekend trip to a B&B and explore the surroundings.
- Have a night picnic in your backyard with candles and soft music.
- Cook a meal together.
- Play music and dance together when no one else is home.

Living with someone else can be hard. You may want to demonstrate the values in 1 Peter 3:8 with your spouse, but something gets in your way. If your spouse has hurt you and there hasn't been good repair, resentment can build and shut your best intentions down. You may be struggling with shame from something in your past or present that keeps you distant. But it's so important to be the safe person for your spouse—the person with whom they can truly be themselves. Intimacy thrives where there is empathy and vulnerability, while disconnection and isolation rule when there's pride, judgment, and shame.

This quiz will help you think about the connection between you and your spouse, and whether it's based on the biblical values of compassion and tenderheartedness. Circle your answers.

1. When I open up to my partner and share vulnerable feelings, I usually feel that:
   a) My partner tries to understand me and I feel supported.
   b) My partner appears disinterested and doesn't always listen.
   c) My partner goes into "fix it" mode and gives me opinions or solutions.
   d) I rarely open up to my partner.

2. My partner's way of communicating is:
   a) Letting me know when something is bothering him or her and wanting to talk about it.
   b) Getting quiet and withdrawn, eventually opening up if I pursue.
   c) Getting angry and taking it out on me or staying silent and withdrawn no matter how many times I ask what's wrong.
   d) Unknown to me. I honestly don't know what is going on inside my partner's head much of the time.

3. When my partner and I spend time together or work on joint projects, we:
   a) Enjoy each other's company and work well together for the most part.
   b) Don't really enjoy the same things, but we sometimes make the effort to share each other's hobbies or chores.
   c) Don't agree on what to do or how to do it, so we usually argue.
   d) Rarely spend time alone together.

4. When my partner and I have conflict:
   a) We usually respect each other's opinions and find a compromise, even when we don't agree.
   b) Things may get heated, but we usually come to an understanding and repair any damage we've done in getting there.
   c) We stay stuck in disagreement, with one or both of us feeling angry, hurt, and resentful.
   d) We don't have conflict anymore because one or both of us has given up.

5. In our views on important issues (money, parenting, religion), my partner and I:
    a) Usually agree. We share common morals, values, and ethics.
    b) Sometimes disagree, but we can usually work out a solution.
    c) Rarely agree and we fight a lot.
    d) Can't even discuss important issues.

6. When I share ideas or concerns with my partner:
    a) I feel respected and heard. I can tell my partner anything.
    b) I sometimes feel my partner does not have my best interests in mind.
    c) I don't trust my partner to keep what I say private between the two of us.
    d) I don't share ideas or concerns with my partner.

7. I feel judged and criticized by my partner:
    a) Rarely.
    b) Occasionally.
    c) Often.
    d) Always.

8. My partner and I show each other affection by holding hands, being playful, hugging, or cuddling:
    a) Always.
    b) Often.
    c) Occasionally.
    d) Rarely.

9. Sex with my partner is:
    a) A strong connection even if we may not have as much time or energy for it as we would like.
    b) Satisfying even if it's a little humdrum or routine.
    c) Something we fight about a lot because we don't have it enough.
    d) Nonexistent.

10. Trust in my relationship is:
    a) Rock solid. My partner is the safest place in the world for me.
    b) Sometimes a problem, but we work through it.
    c) A problem. There are certain issues where I cannot trust my partner at all.
    d) Nonexistent. There is no trust in our relationship.

If you circled mostly As, this is a relationship with many strengths. Keep up the good work and focus on staying connected.

Mostly Bs: Your relationship is workable but might lack a deeper connection. You and your partner may need to learn how to open up communication and share more with each other.

Mostly Cs: Your relationship has some problem areas that should be addressed sooner than later. The longer you wait, the harder it will be to bridge the gaps.

Mostly Ds: Your relationship is lacking in several key areas necessary for connection, intimacy, and trust. It is highly recommended that you work with a therapist who is an expert in couples' issues.

No matter how you scored on this quiz, take heart! It requires a lot of skill to make a marriage work well, and most of us were never taught. But skills can be learned, and the work you're doing in this book is a great first step.

REVIEW

Here's a quick review of what we discussed in this chapter:

- God created you for connection with Him and with your spouse.
- You can add "God time" to your day without adding more stress.
- Things that connect you with your spouse include spending quality time together, having fun, and prioritizing physical touch.
- Things that disconnect you from your spouse include secrets, lack of empathy, and criticism.
- Don't let disconnectors hold you back from a biblical marriage based on love, joy, and peace.

TAKE COURAGE AND DO IT

Here are four actions to take during the next week to foster healthy, loving connection with your spouse:

1. Plan a special date night with your spouse. Focus more on being alone together than spending money or creating an elaborate event.
2. Start a ritual of connection to perform when you leave for the day and when you return. Hug and kiss each other hello and goodbye. You may be surprised to see the impact of this over time.
3. Go to bed or wake up thirty minutes earlier than usual, and spend that time cuddling. Enjoy touching each other in affectionate ways and talking. Be playful. If sex is a problem area in your marriage, designate this as a no-sex zone so that it doesn't cause any pressure or resentment. Otherwise, sex is optional. Either way, agree on your expectations beforehand.
4. Reflect on the Marriage Quiz (see pages 38–40) and how you feel about the results. If you or your spouse scored mostly Cs or Ds, don't panic or get discouraged. Pray and ask God for direction, and consider finding a good marriage counselor or coach.

3

CONFLICT

When two people fall in love, they're often swept up in the thrill of a new relationship and don't notice areas that might become problems for them later. This honeymoon phase usually only lasts one to two years, at which point the couple has to learn how to navigate all the ways they think, feel, and act differently. This is when conflict usually intensifies, as the couple realizes this relationship might be harder than they anticipated. A common pitfall of managing conflict is to escalate the situation to get your point across or to avoid it entirely, but God's Word instructs us to lean into conflict with grace, humility, and love. Learning how to handle conflict in a healthy way becomes increasingly important as relationships mature.

▷—♡→

HEALTHY CONFLICT

Conflict is a struggle that arises from a difference in perspective or desires, and it's a natural part of every relationship. When you and your spouse have disagreements, it doesn't mean you have a bad marriage. In fact, well-managed conflict can be a sign of a healthy marriage because it means both of you feel safe enough to speak your minds. God knew that putting people in community would create opportunities for conflict, especially in marriage, and He has given us instruction on how to navigate our differences.

Write out Colossians 3:12-14.

_____

_____

_____

_____

_____

_____

_____

Understanding these verses is key to learning how to handle conflict in a healthy, constructive way. When you and your partner disagree, do you exhibit the virtues the Apostle Paul describes, bearing with the other person and supporting each other's differences while prioritizing the relationship above your individual desires? Or are you quick to anger, lashing out at your spouse and encouraging him or her to withdraw, shut down, or, worse, lie to you to avoid the eruption? If it isn't emotionally safe for your spouse to share openly and honestly, he or she will turn away. If this happens long enough, seeds of bitterness and resentment will almost certainly flourish.

EXERCISE: MANAGING EMOTIONS DURING CONFLICT

When you think of having conflict, what physical sensations do you experience (sweating, tightness in chest, lump in throat)?

What feelings do you associate with those physical sensations (fear, anxiety, dread)?

What did you learn about conflict from your family while you were growing up? Was it loud? Did someone get hurt? Was there always a winner and a loser?

How do you manage strong emotions when you're in a conflict? Check all that apply:

- ❑ I get angry and yell.
- ❑ I feel flooded with emotions and cannot think clearly.
- ❑ Sometimes I really blow my top and say hateful things.
- ❑ I want the conversation to be over quickly, so I shut it down or leave.
- ❑ I don't want to talk about it.
- ❑ I feel I can't do anything right.
- ❑ I hate conflict and would rather go along to get along.
- ❑ I can be bossy and demanding.
- ❑ I'm afraid of my spouse's reaction, so I tiptoe around tricky subjects.
- ❑ I don't try to find a solution that works for both of us.
- ❑ I don't feel like I can step away temporarily to self-soothe and come back ready to talk calmly.

If you checked two or more items on the list, you might have trouble engaging in conflict in a healthy way. It's important for you to learn the skills to emotionally regulate and experience the tension of conflict without collapsing and giving in or bullying your way through.

How do you experience your spouse when he or she has strong emotions? Check all that apply:

- ❑ My spouse gets angry and yells.
- ❑ My spouse seems to feel his or her way is the right way and lectures me.
- ❑ My spouse shuts the conversation down quickly or walks away.
- ❑ My spouse doesn't want to talk about it, and nothing feels resolved.
- ❑ My spouse gets very critical and says hurtful things.
- ❑ I get scared when my spouse gets really angry.
- ❑ My spouse often gives me the silent treatment when things don't go well.
- ❑ My spouse avoids conflict by not having an opinion.

- [ ] My spouse can be bossy and demanding.
- [ ] My spouse seems to tiptoe around subjects and is often vague.
- [ ] My spouse blows his or her top easily.
- [ ] My spouse rarely takes a time-out to calm down before coming back to a conversation.

If you checked two or more items on the list, your spouse likely has trouble emotionally regulating.

Compare your answers. Are there any surprises? If this exercise brings up strong feelings, I encourage you to be open to the idea that we all have blind spots and this could be an opportunity for both of you to grow and bear with one another. Try not to get angry with your spouse or punish him or her for being honest. This is an excellent opportunity for you both to start practicing new skills that will promote growth.

THE SQUEEZE IS WORTH THE JUICE

Write out Ephesians 4:31–32.

_____

_____

_____

_____

A client once told me he avoided conflict because "the squeeze isn't worth the juice." He felt it wasn't productive and never ended well. It's tempting to want to avoid conflict altogether, but scripture points out how facing conflict appropriately is helpful and necessary. In fact, disagreements (when handled appropriately) can keep things interesting and be the juice that keeps the passion in your marriage alive. Here are a few ways healthy conflict can be good for us:

1. **Healthy conflict strengthens us.** Every change, even a small one, is painful to some degree, but we often grow through that pain. I once heard a story about a boy who noticed a butterfly struggling to free itself from its cocoon. In an attempt to help, he gently pulled the cocoon open, but the butterfly that emerged was shriveled and unable to fly. His teacher explained that as butterflies struggle out of their cocoons, the pressure forces the water from the wings, enabling them to fly. Removing the struggle actually hurts the butterfly. Paul writes, "For Christ's sake, I delight in weaknesses, in insults, in hardships, in persecutions, in difficulties. For when I am weak, then I am strong" (2 Corinthians 12:10). Our struggles can make us feel weak, but God tells us our weaknesses make us strong.

2. **Healthy conflict strengthens our spouses.** Few things help us grow more than to be in a relationship with someone who loves us enough to tell us the truth. Luke 17:3 tells us, "If your brother or sister sins against you, rebuke them; and if they repent, forgive them." If you aren't willing, in a gentle and nonjudgmental way, to hold up a mirror for your spouse, you're missing opportunities for both of you to grow.

3. **Healthy conflict strengthens our relationships.** Avoiding conflict may seem to be the best way to keep the peace, but it's actually unhealthy for our marriages because it builds anxiety, resentment, and contempt. When faced with conflict, it's important not to cave in too quickly to avoid the tension or to overpower our spouses to get our own ways. When two people feel safe enough to firmly stand their ground, it is a sign of a healthy relationship. In Galatians 2:11, Paul takes Peter to task for not eating with Gentiles, but in 2 Peter 3:15–16, Peter speaks highly of Paul's ministry, showing the strength of their friendship despite (or perhaps because of) conflict.

Having a strong visual representation of you at your best can help you emotionally regulate when you're getting angry or feeling threatened during conflict. Review the hurtful and healthy communication habits on pages 10 and 15. Think of the traits you wish to embody when conflict occurs, such as being calm, wise, patient, rational, kind, or fair. (If you have trouble thinking of traits, think about how you handle yourself at work or at church. These are places where we're more likely to show our best selves.)

List seven to ten of those traits here.

Draw a picture of something that symbolizes those traits for you, like an object, an animal, or a person. I had one client who drew the Superman symbol to represent bravery. Another client drew a lion to symbolize strength and dignity. Don't worry if you aren't an artist—the important thing is that drawing accesses a different part of the brain that will help you remember the image.

Give the image you drew a name, one you can recall later with a word or simple phrase. (For example, my client named his lion "Aslan.")

TAKE A BREATHER

Taking a time-out is a powerful therapeutic tool that can be very helpful in defusing arguments. However, many people use time-outs inappropriately to avoid difficult conversations or ignore or punish their spouses. To use time-outs effectively, follow these five rules of engagement:

1. **Decide how long a time-out will last before you use it.** It should be no less than 30 minutes and no more than 24 hours. (If you miss the agreed-upon timeline for reconnection, your spouse might be reluctant to agree to future time-outs.)

2. **When your partner calls a time-out, immediately stand down.** There should be no arguing, words of contempt, or eye rolling. Don't follow your spouse from room to room. Simply thank them for taking care of themselves and the relationship.

3. **During the time-out, take time for reflection.** Answer the following questions: What am I feeling *besides* angry? What is one thing I want my spouse to know about this situation? What am I doing or saying that's making it harder for my spouse to listen? Recall your image of your "best self" and ask yourself how you can act the way God would like you to act.

4. **When the time-out is over, whoever initiated it should reengage.** At that point, both partners should share their answers to the questions you've reflected on. Apologize for your part in the conflict. Assure your spouse of your love and try again. If more time-outs are required, take them.

5. **If time-outs don't work, consider getting professional help.** If you're unable to have a calm discussion after several attempts at time-outs, it may be time to find a good marriage counselor.

We get in trouble when emotions flood over us before our brains can catch up. Calling that pictorial prompt to mind when you start to feel even the slightest sensation of annoyance can be enough to remind you to approach the situation as your best self, the way God wants you to. It sometimes helps to put the picture and/or name on your bathroom mirror as a reminder.

UNHEALTHY CONFLICT STYLES

We tend to engage in conflict based on our individual personality styles. The following are three of the most common styles I see in therapy and descriptions of each one. All of us exhibit each of these personality traits to some degree, and each style has its strengths and weaknesses. The goal is not to label yourself or your partner, but to increase your understanding of what motivates certain approaches to conflict so that you know where to make changes.

PLEASERS

Strengths: Pleasers are easy to get along with and have a strong desire for connection. They are quick to forgive and don't usually hold grudges. They are often the first to apologize in order to restore peace and harmony. They tend to see the good in others.

Weaknesses: Pleasers avoid conflict because they can't tolerate the anxiety they feel when they're in opposition to someone they care about. They often keep silent about their wants, ideas, or opinions for fear of upsetting someone else, which can feel flat or cold to their partners. Pleasers frequently overcommit because they don't want to disappoint anyone, but then find themselves in trouble when they can't deliver on all they've promised. Of all the styles, pleasers seem to be the nicest, but they can have a bad habit of lying or telling partial truths to avoid someone else's anger or disappointment.

Write out Galatians 1:10.

The Bible reminds us to focus on pleasing God; we're not asked to change our behavior to please other people.

AVOIDERS

Strengths: Avoiders are often very task-oriented and often are high achievers. They avoid drama, are usually even-keeled, and seek solutions to problems.

Weaknesses: Avoiders stay away from conflict because they aren't comfortable with messy emotions. But unlike pleasers, avoiders aren't striving for deep emotional connection. In fact, the less you need from them, the better. An avoider often views his or her spouse as too needy or soft and may even show contempt when a spouse expresses the desire for more connection. Avoiders often suppress their own emotions, wanting not to dwell on thoughts that cause them sadness or pain. As a result, they struggle with empathy. They can often be passive-aggressive because it allows them an indirect way to show their frustration. Avoiders often feel smothered by their partner's needs for connection.

The Biblical View:

Write out Ecclesiastes 3:4-5.

This verse tells us that all emotions are a part of life. No matter how hard we try, we can't truly avoid them.

CONTROLLERS

Strengths: Controllers get things done! They take the lead, organize events, and turn ideas into projects. They don't shy away from difficult situations or conversations and are often protective of the ones they love.

Weaknesses: Controllers attempt to contain chaos or uncertainty by managing everyone else instead of managing their own anxiety—although they often don't recognize that they're anxious or controlling. They can also struggle with empathy if they're in task mode, becoming upset if someone doesn't do things the "right" way. Controllers often handle conflict from an authoritarian angle, taking action without consulting others. They can be intimidating because they appear confident, tend to lecture others, and can get angry easily. Controllers often express their anxiety through anger, which relieves some of the pressure they feel. When the blowup is over, they feel better and wonder why everyone else isn't as quick to get over it.

The Biblical View:

Write out Matthew 6:34.

This verse reminds us that, ultimately, God is the one in control, not us.

Which of the conflict styles do you exhibit most when in a conflict with your spouse: pleasing, avoiding, or controlling?

What does your approach look like, specifically? What are you trying to accomplish? What are you trying *not* to do?

How do you feel about this approach? What, if anything, would you like to change?

What positive impact would such a change make?

Which of the conflict styles do you think your spouse mostly exhibits when in a conflict: pleasing, avoiding, or controlling?

How do you respond to your spouse's approach?

What, if anything, would you like your spouse to change in how he or she approaches conflict?

What positive impact do you think it could have if your spouse changed that approach?

HOW TO PROTECT YOURSELF IN A CONFLICT

You are the only person you have any control over. You may be handling conflict in the most healthy, respectful way possible, and your partner still might be unable or unwilling to hold themselves together. It is important to know how to de-escalate a situation or when to remove yourself from one until things are calmer. Here are some strategies to help you do that:

1. **Keep a cool head.** Proverbs 15:1 states that a soft word turns away wrath and a harsh word stirs up anger. Things will go a lot better if at least one of you can stay calm when the heat is on. Too often, we engage in verbal warfare and feed off each other's anger. If your spouse is going off the rails, it may help to say something like: "Honey, I love you and I want to work this out with you, but right now I'm shutting down because of the anger. Please lower your voice so that I can hear you without getting defensive."

Write out Proverbs 15:18.

_____

_____

_____

2. **Set good boundaries.** Boundaries are your personal rules about what you find acceptable or unacceptable. They might be mundane and small like: "I won't wash any laundry that is left on the floor instead of in the hamper." Or they might be more serious like: "If you start yelling, I will leave the room until we can discuss things calmly." In Luke 17:3, God tells us to speak up when others cross our boundaries and to make repair when we cross those that others have set.

Write out Luke 17:3.

_____

_____

_____

3. **Respectfully disengage.** There's a saying I like: "You don't have to attend every argument to which you are invited." When your partner is being unreasonable, argumentative, or mean-spirited, step away. It may mean refusing to engage verbally or leaving the physical space for a time until things calm down. (Note: If you're in a situation where there is domestic violence, please leave the situation until your spouse has gained control of his or her anger. Your safety comes first. See the Resources section on page 150 for help dealing with abuse.)

Write out James 1:19.

_____

_____

_____

Every couple fights sometimes, and my husband and I are no exception. Early on in our marriage, I developed the bad habit of ending stalemates by saying, "Maybe we should just divorce!" I never truly meant those words, but they hurt my husband. We ended up making a contract that said mentioning divorce during a fight was no longer allowed, and I've kept that promise ever since.

Use the template that follows to write your own contract for what is no longer allowed during a fight. Some ideas include cursing, name-calling, threatening divorce, throwing things, giving the other person the silent treatment, and leaving the house. Both of you should start out by choosing no more than two to three things so that you'll more easily remember what they are.

I, _____ , promise not to engage in the following behaviors when we are fighting.

Signed, your loving spouse,

CASE STUDY: MIKE AND TARA

Mike and Tara had regular fights that often escalated into shouting matches or long periods of silence and withdrawal. Tara had a "controller" conflict style. When she got hurt, she got angry, and when she got angry, she yelled insults, threw things, and made hateful comments that hurt Mike. Mike's conflict style was more avoidant. He tiptoed around, trying not to poke the bear. He often lied to Tara to avoid her anger—which only made things worse when she found out about whatever he was hiding.

Before this couple could begin to heal, we had to start with a contract of conduct. Tara promised to stop raging and making hurtful comments. Mike promised to stop lying to cover up mistakes and to start discussing his feelings more. It took this couple several weeks to learn to emotionally regulate themselves enough to keep these promises, but once their destructive behavior was curtailed, they began to be able to negotiate, compromise, and find solutions to problems they'd been fighting about for years. They made huge progress just by learning how their conflict styles were adding to the problem and by making a commitment to change.

RECONCILIATION

Relationships are a constant dance of closeness, rupture, distance, and reconciliation. If you skip that last key step, you're stuck with distance. Because conflict in your marriage is unavoidable, it is imperative to know how to resolve it. I'm always surprised at how many couples don't know how to repair ruptures in their relationships. Most people I see in my office simply ignore the rift and live with tension for so long that neither one even remembers what caused it. I've seen couples go weeks living in the same house and not speaking to each other. Eventually, something happens to ease the tension and the couple starts speaking again, but that's not a real resolution. There's still an emotional distance festering below the surface, waiting for the next offense.

The book of Matthew gives us a valuable perspective on reconciling with another person.

Write out Matthew 5:23-24.

_____

_____

_____

_____

In this passage, who is involved in the conflict? Who was offended? What does Jesus command us to do? When is this to be done?

Now write out Matthew 18:15.

_____

_____

_____

_____

In this passage, who is involved in the conflict? Who was offended? What is the command? When is this to be done?

As you can see, Jesus clearly says to attempt reconciliation whether you're the offender or the offended. It doesn't matter to Him who caused the offense. He puts the responsibility of reconciliation on *both* of you. If you're staying silent and waiting for an apology, you're disobeying God's command.

HOW TO MAKE REPAIR

Making a proper repair requires three steps:

1. **Confess.** The first step is to acknowledge your mistake in a humble and mature manner. Don't let pride keep you from owning your part of the conflict. Some people feel that if they take ownership, they'll end up taking all the blame and letting their partner off the hook. But the truth is that no matter who's at fault, both parties have almost always contributed to the rupture in some way, even if it's simply by a negative or unhelpful reaction.

Write out James 5:16.

_____

_____

_____

_____

2. **Apologize.** It can be hard to apologize sometimes. Some people view it as a sign of weakness or fear it will be used against them somehow. Often, people simply don't feel they've done anything wrong. But apologizing doesn't necessarily mean you've failed or made a mistake. Apologizing can simply be an acknowledgement that your spouse is hurting, which can open the door for reconciliation.

Gary Chapman, author of *The Five Love Languages*, also cowrote *The Five Languages of Apology* with Jennifer Thomas. The book identifies five languages of apology: expressing regret, accepting responsibility, making restitution, genuinely repenting, and requesting forgiveness. Knowing your own and your spouse's "apology language" can be very helpful in restoring and maintaining peace in your home. If you struggle with apologies, reflect on why that may be. Do you have trouble being wrong? Is your pride stopping you?

Write out Proverbs 13:10.

3. **Forgive.** The Bible has a lot to say about forgiveness. It's the foundation of our relationship with God, and it's crucial to our joy, happiness, and spiritual health. Forgiveness is the very essence of God's grace and mercy. God doesn't just suggest we forgive—He commands it.

Write out Matthew 6:14-15.

Because it is commanded, we know that forgiveness is a choice that is *not* based on feelings. We may have to fall on our knees before God to ask for the strength to do it, but it is for His glory and our sanctification that we forgive. Forgiveness does not mean excusing an offense as trivial or unimportant. It does not mean minimizing your pain or giving your spouse a pass to continue to hurt you. Forgiveness is recognizing that the human condition often leaves us predisposed to sinful desires. It is knowing that we all sin and fall short (Romans 3:23). Forgiveness isn't a one-and-done decision; it happens over time. You may have to work at forgiveness every time a negative thought or feeling arises when you think of the offending event.

EXERCISE: PRACTICING FORGIVENESS

Think of someone or something you're struggling to forgive. What is holding you back from forgiving?

Write a prayer to God asking Him to relieve you of the burden of unforgiveness. Ask Him to remove any barriers between you and the freedom of forgiveness.

Write out Luke 6:27–28, then say a prayer of blessing over the person who hurt you.

REVIEW

Here's a quick review of what we discussed in this chapter:

- All marriages have some level of conflict. Healthy conflict strengthens you, your spouse, and your relationship.
- There are three main unhealthy styles of conflict: pleasing, avoiding, and controlling.
- Managing your emotions is important to healthy conflict. Stay calm, set boundaries, and respectfully disengage if things get too heated.
- God commands us to forgive and to reconcile with each other. Reconciliation involves confessing your mistakes, apologizing for your part in the conflict, and forgiving your spouse for his or her part in the conflict.

TAKE COURAGE AND DO IT

Here are five actions to take during the next week to make sure conflict with your spouse is handled healthily and effectively:

1. Each day, take five minutes to visualize your best self, using the image and word from page 50. Sit with your eyes closed and imagine how it would feel to show up like that in a conflict with your spouse. Notice the physical sensations that come with this exercise. Imagine that you can put on and take off your best self like a cloak. It is yours whenever you want it, always accessible.
2. Spend time with the Lord asking Him to reveal to you where conflict is a problem for you. Ask Him for help and guidance to keep your anger in check and to help you speak up respectfully.
3. Set up a time-out ritual with your spouse. Go over the rules and set up the time frames for reconnection that you both can agree on.

4. Try to be the first one to make a repair after a disagreement. If the mood is right, you can make a game of this: the first one to apologize wins!
5. Discuss with your spouse which languages of apology are the most significant to you and why.

Note: If, even after working through this chapter, you find you're having heated disagreements that seem to be escalating, I encourage you to reach out for professional help. A home filled with unhealthy conflict is damaging to everyone, especially your children.

PARTNERSHIP

If I could sum up a healthy marriage in one word, it would be "partnership." Partnership is more than just getting along with each other. It's combining individual strengths and skills for the good of each person and of the couple as a unit. It's a commitment to pursue shared goals with respect for each person's contribution. The relationship between a husband and wife is the only earthly relationship for which the Bible instructs to love as Christ loved the church. There is no other human relationship where God joins two lives together in a holy covenant. If you approach marriage like a true partnership, there is unlimited capacity for love, joy, and peace. Let's look at the cornerstones of effective partnership.

SUBMISSION AND EQUALITY

This first cornerstone of a healthy partnership is often the most misunderstood: submission. We live in a tough era for couples. There are so many mixed messages about the roles of men and women in our world. Men are encouraged to be vulnerable and sensitive, but they're then chided when they're "weak" and told to "man up." Women are supposed to be strong and independent but are also under tremendous pressure to be perfect wives and mothers and to look good doing it. In a world that continues to redefine submission and equality, it is fortunate the Bible gives us guidance on what our roles are in marriage.

THE TRUE MEANING OF SUBMISSION

Write out Ephesians 5:22–24.

_____

_____

_____

_____

Many people interpret this scripture to mean the husband is dominant over the wife, and frankly, this can be a dangerous belief. I've seen husbands who bully, humiliate, and abuse their wives because they feel entitled to bring them into submission. Oh, how this must grieve our Father! The scripture states that husbands are to "love your wives and never treat them harshly" (Colossians 3:19 NLT).

True submission can never be forced. Scripture does not support the idea that the man is a tyrant who rules from an authoritarian mind-set, exerting control through power and coercion. In fact, scripture shows us the perfect example of headship through Christ. If the husband is the head of the wife as Christ is the head of the church, then the husband will be "the leader . . . who serves," who journeys alongside his wife, showing her grace, compassion, love, and respect (Luke 22:26 ESV). Christ was a true servant leader who demonstrated his headship by washing his disciples' feet.

Write out 1 Corinthians 7:4.

_____

_____

_____

Submission is a vital part of our Christian walk. We submit to Christ—and in marriage, we submit to each other. There is an expectation for *all* believers to put aside their pride and preferences for the sake of others. When both wife and husband practice humble submission, there is so much more capacity for joy and peace in the marriage.

SUBMISSION AND THE TRINITY

Write out 1 Corinthians 11:3.

_____

_____

_____

This verse clearly states that man is the head of woman. It also clearly states that God is the head of Christ. What does this mean in terms of equality? Jesus is part of the Godhead, but he is not "equal" to God. There is equality in terms of their value, but their functions and roles are different. God is the head in the function of authority, but the Trinity is a complementary relationship that partners together in unity.

Now write out Philippians 2:5-6.

Likewise, husbands and wives are given distinguishing roles in marriage, but one partner is not superior to the other. Just like the Trinity, marriage is also a complementary relationship of mutual submission.

EXERCISE: WHAT DOES SUBMISSION MEAN TO YOU?

Discuss the following questions with your spouse:

What were each of you taught about the concept of submission and equality in marriage?

Who made most of the decisions in your family of origin? How did the arrangement work?

Was servant leadership modeled for you in your home? How so?

In what ways have you voluntarily submitted yourself to your spouse?

Where can you do better in submitting to your spouse?

Ask your spouse what he or she would like to see you do more of or less of, regarding submission.

LOVE AND RESPECT

Write out Ephesians 5:33.

According to this verse, what is asked of husbands? What is asked of wives? The scripture obviously doesn't mean wives aren't supposed to love their husbands or husbands aren't supposed to respect their wives. I think it's distinguishing between the basic needs each partner has in marriage. Men often tend to feel most loved when they are shown respect from their wives, and women often tend to feel more loved when they are treated as precious and given preference.

One activity that increases feelings of both love and respect is sharing appreciation for one another. We show God our love when we "give thanks to the Lord" and "make known his deeds" (1 Chronicles 16:8 ESV). Showing regular appreciation to our spouses is also important, regardless of gender or who's doing what task. When I got married, I assumed my role was to take care of grocery shopping, cooking, and cleaning, while my husband's role was to take care of all things mechanical and all the yardwork. We realized quickly this wasn't working for us, and I'm grateful I married a sensible, flexible man who was willing to negotiate the chores, especially once we became parents.

EXERCISE: THOSE THINGS YOU DO

Make a list of three to five things your spouse does or says that make you feel loved and respected.

Turn toward your partner, look him or her in the eye, hold hands, and describe what he or she does or says that makes you feel loved and respected. How does it make you feel to say and hear these things? Cherished, important, safe, wanted? Express your appreciation for these efforts.

FINDING A MIDDLE GROUND

Partnership is about mutual respect, servant leadership, and voluntarily submitting to one another unselfishly. Understanding how to find the middle ground in a disagreement is the key to effective partnership.

SHOWING APPRECIATION

Showing appreciation has to come from a grateful heart that sees and acknowledges our spouse's efforts to show us love and respect. It's easy to get busy and take each other for granted. These are some everyday actions that deserve appreciation and gratitude but may go unnoticed:

- Washing and folding laundry
- Making the kids' lunch
- Making the kids' doctor appointments
- Picking up food for dinner
- Buying gifts for friends or family
- Planning a date night
- Remembering a special day
- Running an errand
- Preparing the taxes
- Hosting family on holidays
- Giving your spouse time alone for self-care

- Paying the monthly bills
- Planning a family vacation
- Shopping for school supplies
- Putting gas in the car
- Calling to let you know he or she is running late
- Putting down the phone to have undisturbed conversation
- Making coffee in the morning
- Cleaning up the kitchen
- Taking out the trash

REACHING A COMPROMISE

Write out Ephesians 2:14.

Compromising means meeting in the middle. Both partners give up some, but not all, of what they want. For instance, if you want to spend your savings on a new car and your spouse wants to spend it on a vacation, a compromise might be for you to buy a used car while your spouse spends money on a weekend getaway.

Write out Proverbs 11:1.

Sometimes you'll be faced with a dispute you either can't or simply won't compromise on. This is when it helps to know the art of negotiation. When you negotiate, each of you gets something *you* really want in exchange for giving your partner something *he* or *she* really wants. So to return to the example of the new car and the vacation, you might give up the new car and go on vacation like your spouse wants, but your spouse also agrees to take a second job or otherwise save money for a new car the next year. Both of you get exactly what you want, but it costs you both something. Your cost in this scenario is delayed gratification. Your spouse's cost is the time and effort of a second job.

I love to see couples negotiate, because it requires both partners to be actively engaged in expressing their desires without being too controlling or too passive. When compromising, pleasers and more passive people usually give in too soon in order to avoid conflict and keep the peace. Couples who negotiate well often have healthier marriages because they're not afraid to experience the tension of disagreement long enough to work out a solution.

EXERCISE: DEVELOPING NEGOTIATION SKILLS

Before any negotiation starts, ask yourself these questions:

- What do I want that is different from what my partner wants (chore splitting, time alone, a vacation, etc.)?
- On a scale of 1 to 10, how important is this to me?
- Why is this important? What would getting this mean to me?
- To get what I want, what would be required of my partner?
- What could I offer my partner to make it easier for him or her to agree?
- How would my partner possibly benefit by giving me what I want?

During negotiation, use these strategies to have a productive and effective conversation:

- Review the skills you learned in Chapters 1 through 3 on communicating and connecting.
- Visualize sharing your answers to the above questions with your partner as your highest self.
- Schedule a time to talk.
- Pray together before you enter a negotiation that God will give you both wisdom and guidance.
- Keep your cool no matter what. Negotiating may be a new skill for you both. Not all negotiations go the way we want.

AT AN IMPASSE

What happens when you simply cannot agree and all efforts at negotiation fail?

Write out Proverbs 19:11.

CASE STUDY: SAM AND KIARA

Sam and Kiara came to see me because they were on the verge of separating. Their fights were beginning to escalate in ways that scared them both. Kiara said she dreaded Sam coming home from work every day because they almost always found something to argue about. Sam would distance himself by going upstairs and watching TV or playing video games, leaving Kiara alone to take care of the kids. Sam dreaded coming home after work because he felt Kiara's complaints started the minute he walked in. The more she complained, the more he distanced himself. The more he distanced himself, the more she complained. They were locked in a toxic cycle.

I gave them the same homework assignment every week for the first several months: They each had to share one appreciation with each other, every night. They were amazed at how quickly this exercise changed their pattern of complaint and withdrawal. I could tell each week in our session whether they had been doing the exercise by their demeanor and attitude. When they shared appreciations, they reported a positive week with a lot of progress. When life got busy and they didn't do so, they reported more tension and irritability at home.

The Bible says that it's to a person's "glory" to overlook an offense. That means that when we come to an impasse, instead of getting offended and storming off, we can choose a better path.

Coming to an impasse is a tough situation for any couple, but it happens. In my marriage, my husband and I have negotiated who will have authority or "headship" over different aspects of our lives. I run a large counseling practice, and I sometimes have to make decisions that also affect my husband regarding my time and our finances. I always take his wants and needs into consideration, but if we reach an impasse, I have the deciding vote. My husband has authority over much of the running of our home and cars. He once wanted to purchase a riding lawn mower when I felt it wasn't necessary. He got the deciding vote. This works for us because we both practice submission to one another, even as we have to make difficult choices sometimes.

When deciding who is going to have authority over a particular area, it's important to consider each of your interests, gifts, and skills. We all have to do things sometimes we aren't interested in or aren't particularly good at, but if we leverage the combined talents of the partnership, we get more traction with less stress.

EXERCISE: AREAS OF AUTHORITY

Which of the following areas fall under your interests, skills, or gifts and which fall under your spouse's?

	MINE	YOURS	BOTH	NEITHER
FINANCES				
Paying bills				
Budgets				
Taxes				
HOME				
Grocery shopping				
Cooking				
Cleaning up kitchen				
Laundry				
Ironing				
Vacuuming				
Cleaning bathrooms				
Dusting				
Home maintenance and repair				

	MINE	YOURS	BOTH	NEITHER
Home insurance				
Lawn/garden				
AUTOS				
Routine maintenance				
Handling repairs				
Getting insurance				
OTHER				
Planning vacations				
Planning holiday celebrations				
Helping kids with homework				
Getting kids to and from school				
Buying gifts				
ADD YOUR OWN				

If you chose "both" or "neither" for any of these tasks, this is a good time to begin practicing the negotiation skills you learned in the previous exercise. By the time you're finished with this exercise, you will have determined whose authority will stand when an impasse occurs between you. Remember, having authority does not mean you don't carefully consider your spouse's feelings and desires. Servant leaders negotiate from an unselfish position in accordance with God's commands.

REVIEW

Here's a quick review of what we discussed in this chapter:

- The cornerstones of marital partnership include submission, equality, love, respect, compromise, and negotiation.
- Submission is a mutual responsibility for both husbands and wives, and it never means to dominate over or force our wills on each other.
- Men are given the headship role in marriage, and Jesus showed us that headship is servant leadership rather than a dictatorship.
- Both husbands and wives want respect and love, but husbands are more likely to be driven by the need for respect and wives by the need to feel loved.
- You must be skilled at both compromise and negotiation for your marital partnership to function effectively. It is wise to mutually agree on who has authority over specific areas of domestic life.

TAKE COURAGE AND DO IT

To jump-start your partnership, consider the following over this next week:

1. Pray together for God to give you humble, receptive hearts and the wisdom to build a new foundation of mutual submission to each other and to Him.
2. Begin giving your spouse daily appreciations for the gifts he or she brings to your marriage.

3. Discuss the idea of mutual submission. Consider these questions: How do you feel about the idea of mutual submission? What are some of the benefits you would see in your marriage if you committed to it? What are some of the challenges you anticipate from mutually submitting?

4. Give each other a lot of high fives for the changes you're making, even the small ones. Any change is hard, and the more we acknowledge and encourage, the easier it is to be consistent.

5. Some things shouldn't be compromised or negotiated, including core values, spirituality, emotions, and trust. Discuss what things you consider nonnegotiable and why.

5

FAMILY

From Cain and Abel to Ruth and Naomi, the Bible shows us that families can be a source of both great distress and great joy. Families are complex and multidimensional, and to maintain joy, love, and peace in our homes, we have to practice grace, humility, and submission. What better way to begin to grasp our Heavenly Father's love for us? When you get married, not only do you have to learn how to navigate your new role as a husband or wife, you also have to redefine roles with your family of origin and with your in-laws. That's a lot of learning and adjustment, but the Bible can help guide us through it.

▷—♡→

YOUR FAMILY OF ORIGIN

Our family of origin is where we begin to understand and relate to others. We inherit certain physical traits from our biological parents, but we also inherit emotional and psychological traits from those who raised us (biological parents or not). It's important to understand our emotional genetics because our past wires us and affects how we interact in the present and future.

The home you grew up in sets the stage for the person you become, but it doesn't have to define you. You get to choose what to keep from your family legacy and what to let go. Please know this lesson is not designed to place blame on your parents. Most parents do the best job they can with the tools they have. The goal of this chapter is to understand the background we bring into our marriages, both positive and negative, so that we can create the healthiest possible family relationships.

There are two primary commandments in the Bible that instruct us on how to relate to our parents: We are told to honor our parents and also to leave them once we're married.

Let's take a closer look at both.

THE PAST: HONOR YOUR PARENTS

Write out Ephesians 6:1–3.

Honoring your parents is much easier for some than for others. If you grew up in a home where you were consistently nurtured, loved, and accepted, honoring your parents probably feels natural. Unfortunately, not everyone has this experience. I'm not sure anything causes us more pain than growing up with abuse or neglect. God knows this, yet He still instructs us to honor our parents. How do we obey this commandment if our parents were abusive or neglectful? Honoring your parents does not mean allowing abuse to continue or doing everything they want.

Here are some specific ways you can honor even abusive parents:

1. Pray for them. Ask God to bless your parents and to help you release any resentments or hurt you have held close from your childhood.
2. Forgive them. Remember that Jesus commands us to forgive each other "not seven times, but seventy-seven times" (Matthew 18:21–22). Review the lesson about forgiveness on pages 63–65 in Chapter 3.
3. Reconcile. Instead of responding to abuse with more abuse, "so far as it depends on you, live peaceably with all" (Romans 12:18 ESV). Sometimes distancing yourself from your parents is necessary, but completely withdrawing should be rare and only in extreme circumstances.
4. Provide for them. Make sure your parents have the basic necessities to live, including shelter, food, and healthcare. Check in to make sure they're getting what they need.
5. Love them. Jesus taught us to "love your enemies" and "pray for those who abuse you" (Luke 6:27–28 ESV). This will be tough if your parents were unable to show you the love you deserved, but trust that God will help you do it. In fact, I've only been able to love the "unlovable" when I relied on God's strength and wisdom to show me how.

In this exercise, you'll make a generational map that details some of your family's emotional and psychological DNA. Draw a family tree depicting your grandparents, your parents, you, and your siblings. Starting with your grandparents, write down three positive things you remember or know about each of them. Also list three negative things. If you're aware of any addictions or abusive behavior, note that, as well. Repeat the process for your parents and siblings. Do you see any patterns flowing through the generations? Can you see how the traits of your grandparents influenced your parents and then you?

Discuss your observations with your spouse. Your spouse may see things you miss, so be open to input here. Decide which patterns you want to change, and discuss with your spouse how you plan to change them.

This exercise can be painful for some people. Give each other a big hug and reassurance that patterns are not inevitable. "Nothing will be impossible with God" (Luke 1:37 ESV). He can change any situation if you give Him permission to work in your life.

If you experienced emotional, verbal, physical, or sexual abuse as a child, I recommend getting trauma therapy. Not all trauma is extreme. If you had a parent who was an addict or simply wasn't available, it can leave you with fairly significant baggage that will affect the way you act as a spouse and parent. Get the help that will assist you in redrawing your genealogical map.

THE PRESENT: LEAVING AND CLEAVING

Write out Genesis 2:24.

When you get married, you're not just "cleaving to" your spouse, as the King James Version puts it—you're also leaving your parents. That doesn't mean you and your parents aren't part of each other's lives. It means you and your spouse are two independent adults building your own family unit. It means no one should come between you and your spouse, not even your parents. I see a lot of marital conflict that could be avoided if parents stopped "helping" (meddling with) their adult children and/or if the adult children stopped being financially or emotionally dependent on their parents. Depending on your parents to pay your bills or listen to you complain about your spouse impedes the bond you're building with your spouse.

The best way to be independent from your parents while still obeying the command to honor them is to establish good, healthy boundaries. Boundaries are limits you place on yourself. For example, I can't stop you from insulting me, but I can set a boundary by removing myself from the situation when you do. People sometimes misunderstand boundaries and think they're mean or rude, but I strive to educate my clients that boundaries *protect* relationships. Understanding how and when to use them can save difficult relationships.

This quiz will help you assess whether you're maintaining healthy boundaries with your parents. Circle the appropriate answer for yourself.

1. When my parents want to come over and it isn't a good time, I feel uncomfortable telling them no, so I make adjustments and allow them to come. Yes / No

2. When I'm upset or frustrated with my spouse, I call one or both of my parents to vent. Yes / No

3. Sometimes I get in a financial bind and ask my parents for help. Yes / No

4. One or both parents sometimes say unkind things to me or my spouse, and I either pretend I don't hear it or tell my spouse it isn't a big deal. Yes / No

5. My parents visit without letting us know in advance, and it bothers my spouse. Yes / No

6. When my parents won't babysit or help with my kids, it makes me angry. Yes / No

7. My spouse often feels criticized by my parents. Yes / No

8. My spouse and I go through periods of not speaking to my parents because of the way they treat us. Yes / No

9. I usually ask my spouse to accommodate my parents rather than risk my parents feeling hurt or getting angry. Yes / No

10. Sometimes, my parents take my side when my spouse and I are in a disagreement, and my spouse feels ganged up on. Yes / No

If you answered yes to two or more of these statements, you may have boundary issues with your parents—either not enforcing your own or not respecting theirs. If you don't learn to set healthy boundaries, your spouse can become resentful and lose respect for you. You may think you're protecting your relationship with your parents, but in reality, you're brewing a pot that will eventually boil over and damage your marriage partnership.

HOW TO SET HEALTHY BOUNDARIES

How can you and your spouse set healthy boundaries with your parents?

1. Once you and your spouse have agreed upon a necessary boundary, clearly express it to your parents. Here is an example: "We ask that you call us before you visit, rather than dropping in unexpectedly. We love spending time with you, and planning visits beforehand lets us schedule our time so that we can really enjoy being together."

2. If your parents cross the clearly stated boundary, remind them of your request and ask them to help you maintain this boundary.

3. If your request is repeatedly ignored, ask firmly but politely for the behavior to stop. Further action may also be required. For example, I had one client who changed the locks on his house so that his parents could no longer walk in without knocking. This was an extreme action, but his parents had repeatedly refused to respect the boundary he set. They felt hurt and angry, but by enforcing the boundary, he was actually protecting his relationships with his wife *and* his parents.

4. If the behavior still doesn't stop, limit opportunities for your parents to cross your boundary. For example, if your parents frequently criticize your spouse at holiday gatherings, you might start dropping by for a brief visit but leaving before dinner.

5. Thank your parents when they honor your boundaries.

6. Honor your parents' own boundaries. It's a two-way street. They may not want to keep your kids an entire weekend or come feed your cat when you're away.

IN-LAWS OR OUTLAWS?

Write out 1 Peter 4:8.

_____

_____

When we were newly married, my husband and I were in a small group at church with several other couples our age. I noticed a disturbing trend: Several of the women were regularly bashing their mothers-in-law. I once heard one say, "I always spend Christmas with my parents. His mother doesn't like it, but she has to understand that daughters are closer to their parents than sons." She said this as she held her infant son on her lap, and I had to wonder if she would feel the same way in 20 years.

Feelings like this aren't unusual, but favoring our own parents over our in-laws can be a missed opportunity. Your relationship with your in-laws can be a beautiful experience, even if it gets off to a rocky start. Building families takes time and patience. Make an intentional effort to include your in-laws as much as you include your parents. Send them pictures of their grandchildren. Call them regularly to see how they're doing. Try to develop your own personal relationship with them apart from the one they have with your spouse. If you have a contentious relationship with them, pray for healing and begin to honor them, even when it's hard.

Read Ruth 1:1–17 and discuss with your spouse the relationship between Ruth and Naomi. Share your deepest desires regarding relationships with your parents and your spouse's parents. Are you and your spouse in alignment? What is standing in the way of you having this kind of relationship with your in-laws?

THE PERFECT PARENT

Of course, no matter what our earthly parents are like, we all have a Father in heaven. I've seen people struggle to view God as a Heavenly Father because of their painful relationship with their earthly father (and mother). If you've never had the role of a loving parent modeled for you, it may be difficult to feel safe and loved by God the Father. But, oh, how He loves you. Here are some of the ways the Bible says God parents you:

- You will never lose His love (Psalm 106:1).
- He knows what's best for you and wants to give you whatever you ask for, as long as it's good for you (Romans 8:32).
- He will always be there for you. Nothing can get between you and the Father who loves you (Romans 8:38–39).
- He loves you enough to discipline you (Proverbs 3:11–12). When appropriate discipline comes from the hand of a loving parent, it isn't something to be feared. It isn't abusive or mean-spirited.
- He gives you wisdom (James 1:5).
- He knows you inside and out (Psalm 139:1–3). There is no part of you that you need to hide. He knows all your flaws and He loves you anyway.
- He is always patient and kind (Psalm 103:8). Even good earthly fathers lose their patience, but God never does. You can call on Him anytime, anywhere.
- He loves you unconditionally (Romans 5:8).

In what ways do you struggle with the idea of God as the perfect parent?

Write out a prayer to God thanking Him for the ways He loves you and parents you.

_____

_____

_____

_____

_____

CASE STUDY: ALEX AND CINDY

Alex and Cindy were at the breaking point. Cindy called her mom every time she and Alex had a fight, and then Cindy's mom would email Alex and "advise" him on how to reconcile or make Cindy happy. She called her dad every time she needed a handyman, and he'd show up with his tools. Alex wanted Cindy to stop telling her parents about all their problems, but she thought he was just being too sensitive. She knew her parents loved to help, and she doubted Alex could take care of things without them. It took Cindy a while to realize how her parents' involvement was coming between her and her husband, but eventually she made a change. She had to learn to rely on Alex instead of her parents, which could be tough when one of them messed up or didn't have the skills needed. Her parents didn't understand why Cindy stopped calling as often, and they got upset with her, which bothered her a great deal. But she noticed that as she and Alex became closer, her parents also seemed to respect Alex more. Eventually, the family system recovered and became a much healthier environment for all of them, even though it had a rough start.

REVIEW

Here's a quick review of what we discussed in this chapter:

- The home you grew up in shaped who you are today, but you can choose to keep only what was helpful and let go of the rest.
- The command to honor your parents does not mean giving them preference over your own needs or your spouse's.
- Leaving your mother and father means becoming independent from them emotionally and financially while becoming interdependent with your spouse.
- Kind, respectful boundaries protect all relationships.
- Your in-laws deserve the same consideration as your family of origin. Honor them in the same ways you honor your parents.
- God is the only perfect parent, and you can trust Him to love you and look out for your best interests.

TAKE COURAGE AND DO IT

Here are four actions to take this week to build family relationships full of love, joy, and peace:

1. Set a time to meet with your spouse and discuss areas of conflict with either set of parents. Decide what boundaries need to be set and discuss your plan for communicating these to your family.
2. Discuss the ways you currently honor each other's parents. What are you willing to provide in the future as they age? What are you unwilling to provide?
3. Discuss areas where your boundaries may be too rigid or too relaxed. It can be a challenge to set healthy boundaries, but it's critically important.
4. Discuss areas where you struggle setting boundaries. Sometimes setting boundaries is hard. Discuss what you find difficult about the process. What are you afraid will happen?

6

MONEY

It is often said that money can't buy happiness, but it can certainly provide stability, security, and the freedom to spend time with those you love. Life is hard if you're struggling to make ends meet, and a certain amount of money can at least buy you more opportunities to be happy. However, money also has the potential to buy you misery if you aren't careful. The Bible famously says that the love of money is the root of all evil (1 Timothy 6:10), but it also provides instruction on how we should spend, save, give, and think about money.

MONEY AND VALUES

Write out Matthew 6:24.

_____

_____

_____

In the most basic sense, money is simply a resource that we exchange for what we want and need. We rarely, however, view it that way. Instead, we attach strong, unexamined feelings to it. We might see it as a symbol of our worth, a tool to change the way people treat us, or a form of power over others. Those thoughts can easily become toxic. It's important to figure out what values we place on money and whether or not they align with God's view of money.

EXERCISE: HOW DO YOU FEEL ABOUT MONEY?

Answer the following questions, then compare your answers with your spouse's and discuss.

How was money viewed in your family growing up? Was there an attitude of abundance or scarcity?

_____

_____

_____

How has your past influenced how you view money today?

In what ways are you generous with your money?

In what ways are you fearful about money?

What is one financial area where you want to ask God for more wisdom?

WORKING FOR A LIVING

Write out 2 Thessalonians 3:10.

The Bible tells us to work and to support our own households. Part of being an adult is being financially independent, and unless you have a trust fund, you're going to have to work and earn wages. Some couples struggle to agree on whether both spouses should work or one should stay home. Traditionally, men were employed outside of the home and women worked domestically to care for the family's needs. Today, it is common to find those roles reversed or for both part-ners to earn money. The Bible doesn't specify *who* earns wages—it just says we should avoid being idle.

EXERCISE: WHO WORKS?

Discuss your thoughts and feelings with your spouse about who should work for wages in your home. Where are you in agreement?

Where do you disagree?

FAIR WAGES

James 5:4 reminds us of the importance of paying workers a fair wage. Just because we *can* get someone to do a job for very little pay doesn't mean we *should*. In fact, God tells us to treat others fairly and generously. When we give abundantly, we receive abundantly. What if we applied this concept to our spouses? What is a "fair wage" for the things our spouse does to support the family? Both of you do unpaid work around the home, whether it's mowing the grass, grocery shopping, laundry, or taking care of the kids, but women often do more of the household chores, whether or not they also work outside the home. It's important your spouse feels valued for the ways he or she contributes. What would you do differently if you viewed the work your spouse does at home as deserving of a fair wage and the currency required for payment as respect, gratitude, and appreciation?

What influences your thoughts about the different roles?

How strongly do you feel about this?

GODLY GIVING

Write out 2 Corinthians 9:7.

Our God is so generous with us that it should come as no surprise He instructs us to be generous, too. God doesn't command us to tithe in the New Testament, but tithing is mentioned as the benchmark for giving in the Old Testament. Whatever you choose to give back to the Lord—whether you're giving to your church, to individuals who are in need, or to organizations that do good in the world—you are told to give generously, cheerfully, and intentionally. After all, you're only giving back what came from His hand to begin with, and it all belongs to Him. God doesn't ask you to give to Him because He needs your money. He wants your heart in the right place to foster generosity over greed. In Luke 21:1–4, the widow gave only two mites, but Jesus said she gave more than anyone else because it was all she had. She didn't give out of her abundance but out of her poverty and from a full, grateful heart. How much more would you give back to God if your giving came from this kind of heart?

Discuss your thoughts on tithing and charitable giving with your spouse. How much will you give back to the Lord each month, and where will you give it?

Consider setting up a separate fund solely for the purpose of being generous with others. How much will you commit to put aside for this?

SAVING UP

Write out Proverbs 21:20.

It's harder to be generous if your finances aren't in order, and many Americans aren't saving enough money. The personal-finance website MagnifyMoney reported that 29 percent of households have less than $1,000 in savings, and according to the insurance company Northwestern Mutual, the average American is $38,000 in debt. We aren't preparing—in many cases, *can't* prepare—for our retirement, our kids' college tuitions, or even a basic emergency fund, and we're having a hard time obeying God's command to "let no debt remain outstanding" (Romans 13:8).

It can feel discouraging to work hard to meet your family's needs and prepare for the future, only to find there's not enough money to put in savings. But don't be disheartened! God has promised He will provide for your needs.

Write out Philippians 4:19.

That doesn't mean you shouldn't be financially responsible and independent. In fact, these things let you be a good steward of the blessings God has given you and allow you to give to others. But one of the dangers of money is that independence can become self-reliance. We can easily begin to feel less reliant on God and forget that all good things come from Him. This is the root of the evil God warns us about in 1 Timothy 6:10. Your job is to work hard, be generous, and wisely steward the money you have. God will take care of the rest.

Discuss with your spouse your thoughts on the importance of saving money. Are you in alignment? Are you thoughtfully preparing for the future? If not, why?

_____

_____

_____

_____

Do you worry about money? Why or why not?

_____

_____

_____

_____

Do you feel you're being good stewards of your money? Why or why not?

_____

_____

_____

_____

What is one thing you can do differently with your money that would ease your worries or fears (for example, stick to a budget, cut back on unnecessary expenses, pray for God's provision)?

What can you and your spouse start doing today to approach the way you handle money as a team (for example, schedule a monthly meeting to review your budget together, set spending limits)?

BUDGETING

Write out Luke 14:28.

I love this verse because it shows the wisdom of budgeting! As Jesus pointed out, it's wise to anticipate your expenses and prepare for them. Too many couples aren't diligently tracking their income and expenses, and I've seen it rob them of peace and joy. If your debt or spending is out of control, don't waste time feeling shame or embarrassment. Instead, use that energy to change the situation.

CASE STUDY: MARCO AND ELENA

Marco and Elena came to see me because they were fighting about money. Marco felt Elena spent frivolously and expected him to find ways to make ends meet. Each month when he paid the bills, he ended up so frustrated he'd yell at her and threaten to cut off all the credit cards. Elena was tired of his tirades, so she got a secret credit card. By the time Marco found out about it, Elena had accumulated over $30,000 in debt. This couple didn't find healing until both were ready and able to accept their own faults in the mess. Marco was right to be concerned about Elena's spending, but he reacted in ways that drove disconnection rather than teamwork. If he'd approached her differently and set appropriate boundaries, he probably would have gotten a different outcome. Elena was right to be upset about Marco's temper, but she did betray him when she racked up debt behind his back.

Once they could own their individual parts, they tackled the debt together. Elena cut up all her cards and got a part-time job to pay the balance. Marco kept his cool and began including Elena in monthly budget meetings. Elena was much more willing to stay within certain parameters when she had a say in establishing them. Two years later, they're out of debt and saving money. Marco even says the roles have reversed: Elena is now the avid saver, and he has to convince her to spend a little money on something fun.

EXERCISE: MAKE A BUDGET

To get an accurate idea of what you're currently earning and spending, start by tracking the last three months of your earnings and expenses. Then create a proposed budget for the next month. There are free budget templates online, or you can use the one that follows. I put charitable giving at the top of the list of expenses, thus making it a priority.

	MONTH 1	MONTH 2	MONTH 3	NEXT MONTH
Total Take-home Income (after taxes):				
Church/Charity Contribution				
Rent or Mortgage				
Car Payment				
Utilities				
Phones				
Auto Fuel				
Car and Home Insurance				
Groceries				
Dining Out				
Credit Card Payments				
Student loans				
Medical				
Entertainment				
Childcare				
Clothing				
Vacation				
Gifts				
Retirement Savings				
Regular Savings				
Other Expenses				
Total Expenses				

Subtract your total expenses from your total income to see how much (or how little) you're saving per month: $_____.

Discuss this budget with your spouse. Are there any surprises? In which areas would you like to spend more or less? In which areas would your spouse like to spend more or less?

THE FIVE MOST COMMON MONEY MISTAKES IN MARRIAGES

Write out Proverbs 27:23.

_____

_____

Although the Bible stresses the importance of spiritual riches over material riches, it also advises us to manage our finances wisely. You can't do that within your marriage if you're not working on your finances as a team. Here is a list of the common mistakes I see couples make:

1. Financial infidelity. Hiding money, credit cards, or spending from your spouse is a betrayal. It means you're not partnering in a key area of your marriage. If you're hiding because you're afraid of your spouse's reaction, you may need to see a professional who can help you both see how you're contributing to the problem.
2. Keeping their money separate. Couples usually do this to avoid conflict or to maintain some degree of control that one or both is unwilling to relinquish. I view sharing your finances as an opportunity to learn to negotiate and grow together as a team. Keeping your money separate is not always a mistake—in fact, sometimes it's recommended—but it can be a sign of underdevelopment in the relationship.
3. Unequal partnering. One person may take headship of the finances, but that doesn't mean the other is left in the dark. Even if one of you has no interest in finances, it's prudent for you both to understand where the money is going

and make decisions together on how much to spend. It isn't uncommon for partners to avoid all talks about money. If your spouse won't talk to you about money, use the skills you learned in prior chapters to ask for what you want and to negotiate effectively.

4. **Financial negligence.** I'm often shocked at how little some people pay attention to the "condition of their flocks." If you don't know how much money comes in and goes out each month, you may be financially negligent. You can't be a good steward if you don't know where your money goes. You can monitor your spending and saving with programs like Quicken, Mint, and Everydollar. Be intentional in your giving, saving, and spending.

5. **Living beyond their means.** I promise you'll increase your joy, peace, and happiness if you buy less than you can afford. Two of the biggest culprits here are houses and cars; the bank will almost always approve you for more than is wise to spend. Dave and Sharon Ramsey's book *Financial Peace* recommends your house payment, property tax, and insurance be no more than 25 percent of your take-home pay and that your house payment be a 15-year mortgage.

EXERCISE: GIVE ATTENTION TO YOUR "FLOCKS"

Of the five common mistakes, which ones (if any) apply to you?

_____

_____

Is there anything on this list you feel applies to your spouse?

_____

_____

Discuss your answers, but remember that these are common mistakes and give each other grace. It's a big step to tackle these money issues, and you need to do this as a team. Encourage each other and avoid criticizing. After reviewing your budget, decide on a small amount of spending money you'll each get per month. This is money that doesn't have to be accounted for or explained. You can each do whatever you want with it. (For example, this is how my husband funds his woodworking tools and I fund my clothing budget.)

REVIEW

Here's a quick review of what we discussed in this chapter:

- Money has a lot of symbolism and emotions attached to it, which can tempt us to make it the focus of our desires rather than God.
- Being financially responsible means being intentional with how we earn, spend, give, or save our money.
- We should always be reliant on God rather than ourselves, even as we strive for financial independence.
- It is important to fully engage with our partner when it comes to finances, and to be in alignment with each other's goals and decisions.
- Living below your means is a fast track to peace and joy.

TAKE COURAGE AND DO IT

Here are five actions to take this week to help you and your spouse approach money in a loving, peaceful, and godly way:

1. Look over your budget and see if you can increase your charitable giving, even if it's only by $10 a month.

2. Make a list of all your debts. Include the amounts you owe, the interest rates, and the monthly payment amounts. Put them in order from the lowest amount owed to the highest. Look at the budget you made. How much extra money can you pay on the lowest amount owed while still paying the minimum payments on the rest? You have now started the "debt snowball" repayment plan. Once you pay off the lowest amount, take all that money you were paying and apply it to the next in line. Do this until all debt is paid. Don't get discouraged if the amount you owe is really high. If you work as a team, with God's help, you can do this!

3. If you're in debt, take all your credit cards and put them in the safe-deposit box in your bank, tuck them away somewhere, or cut them up and cancel them. Use Dave Ramsey's "envelope system" to start paying cash for things like groceries and entertainment. This will help you stick to your new budget.

4. Evaluate your current job(s). Are you making a fair wage? If not, is it possible to ask for a raise or find another job that pays more?

5. Discuss ways you can add extra income to your household if you need to increase your cash flow, such as picking up a side job.

SEX

Couples are often shy about discussing sex or the specifics around sexual activity, but the Bible is not squeamish about sex at all. (Just look at the Song of Solomon!) God created us with the capacity for sexual enjoyment, and it is a precious gift that can enhance the marriage relationship if we are responsible and mature enough to give and receive it as God intended.

SEX IS NOT SHAMEFUL

Write out Song of Solomon 1:2.

I've worked with many people who have a distorted view of sex because of a well-intentioned Christian upbringing that placed so much emphasis on remaining sexually pure that it inadvertently sent the message that all sex is shameful or dirty. But God designed our bodies to enjoy sexual touch in the confines of marriage between two consenting adults. Just like anything else, we can make it into something it was never intended to be—and the world's view of sex often *is* shameful. Rape, incest, pornography, adultery, prostitution, and sex trafficking are all distorted versions of the gift God gave us. But God made sex part of His divine plan for the covenant relationship of marriage.

It has three purposes:

1. To produce offspring (Genesis 1:28).
2. To bring pleasure (Proverbs 5:18–19).
3. To increase physical and emotional bonding (Mark 10:8).

Write out Genesis 2:25.

Getting comfortable with your body is an important part of enjoying sex, as it gives you the freedom to experiment with each other without holding back. Giving and receiving physical pleasure is part of God's design for marriage, so don't be shy!

Answer the following questions and discuss your answers with your spouse.
Was sex discussed openly and appropriately in your home growing up? Why or
why not?

Where did most of your sex education come from? Did you feel the information
was adequate or healthy?

Do you feel comfortable discussing sex with your partner? Why or why not?

Is there anything about sex that feels shameful or embarrassing to you? If so, talk to your partner about your feelings and where you received this message.

On a scale of 1 to 10, with 1 being completely uncomfortable and 10 being extremely comfortable, how comfortable are you with your body? If you answered 5 or below, what about your body makes you uncomfortable?

What are you willing and able to do to bring that number up?

SEXUAL TRAUMA

Unfortunately, sexual trauma is not uncommon. The anti–sexual violence organization RAINN reports that 1 in 9 girls and 1 in 53 boys experience sexual assault at the hands of an adult—and those are just the reported cases. Sexual trauma is not limited to physical acts. Children can be sexually traumatized when they are inappropriately exposed to nudity or sexual information. Sexual trauma can happen at any age, but children are the most vulnerable. I see many adults in therapy who were victims of sexual abuse or assault, and their pain is heartbreaking. It's common for survivors to carry some guilt or shame for the abuse even if they know intellectually it was not their fault. If you or your spouse was sexually abused or exploited, please know you are not alone. Don't be embarrassed to reach out to a professional for help with this. This is not your shame to carry; it is your abuser's. You are not broken, soiled, or cast aside. You are a child of God, and you can heal from this.

If your spouse is struggling with sex today because of past sexual trauma, this is a tough situation for you, as well. You may feel helpless or even guilty for wanting a sexual relationship. I encourage you to be patient and loving and gently encourage your spouse to get professional help. If your spouse isn't comfortable going to a counselor over this issue, you may find it helpful to go yourself.

SEXUAL (IN)FREQUENCY

Write out Song of Solomon 7:10.

Many married couples don't have sex as often as they want. There are many reasons people don't have enough sex, including medical conditions and hormonal imbalances, but the majority of people I see struggle for more complicated reasons. I often teach couples the "dual control model" of sexual response (DCM), which says that when it comes to sexual desire, we all have "accelerators" (things that increase our desire) and "brakes" (things that decrease our desire). Everyone's accelerators and brakes are different.

Examples of accelerators:

- Sights (your spouse looks particularly attractive or wears something you like)
- Smells (like cologne)
- Seeing your spouse perform a skill with confidence
- Feeling appreciated, respected, or loved
- Being in a relaxing place or getting away for some time alone
- Watching your spouse interact well with your kids
- Hearing your spouse compliment you to someone else

Examples of brakes:

- Feeling self-conscious about your body or weight
- Not being attracted to your spouse's body
- Poor hygiene
- Feeling criticized by your spouse
- Exhaustion, stress, or illness
- Viewing sex as a burden or chore
- Being busy and distracted
- Anxiety or depression
- Resentment or anger toward your spouse

If you or your spouse "wants to want sex," it is important to assess what activates your desire and what puts on the brakes. Then, make some adjustments. Some people have very sensitive accelerators and experience sexual desire frequently without much thought or effort. Others may have very sensitive brakes and have to work much harder to desire sex.

EXERCISE: ACCELERATORS AND BRAKES

List some of your accelerators and brakes.

Your Accelerators

Your Brakes

Compare your answers with your partner's and answer the following questions together:

What can you do to activate your accelerator?

A NOTE ON PORNOGRAPHY

I can't write a chapter on sex and not address pornography. People often use porn to activate their accelerators with or without their partners, but this is a bad idea. *Your Brain on Porn* is an educational website that describes porn's harmful effects on sexual relationships and mental health. I've worked with couples who could no longer enjoy healthy, "regular" sex because of porn use by one or both partners. Porn isn't just a man's temptation; a survey in *Marie Claire* found that one in three women watch porn at least once a week. Women are also more prone to read romance novels or erotica that can have the same addictive aspects as viewing porn. Addressing sexual issues in a marriage lets couples experience fulfilling sexual pleasure without relying on pornography.

What can your partner do to activate your accelerators?

_____

_____

_____

What can you do to deactivate your brakes?

_____

_____

_____

_____

What can your partner do to deactivate your brakes?

_____

_____

_____

MISMATCHED SEX DRIVES

Write out 1 Corinthians 7:3–5.

_____

_____

_____

_____

_____

_____

_____

It's common for two married partners to have different levels of desire and for those discrepancies to result in conflict, resentment, and anger. I've seen many marriages end unnecessarily over sex because of unmet expectations, inability or unwillingness to negotiate, and the tendency to take "no" as a very personal rejection. It isn't always the woman who has a lower sex drive. In fact, I think it's probably close to 50/50 whether it's the man or the woman who wants sex less.

If you're the "*higher-desire*" *spouse*, it's easy to feel angry and resentful. I don't want to minimize your pain and frustration, but I encourage you not to fall into the common traps that only make this situation worse. These include the following:

Coercing or guilting your spouse into having sex when he or she is not interested. Your spouse may give you what you want, but it can cost you dearly. No one wants to feel controlled, especially in the area of sex. Sex is a gift, but you aren't entitled to receive it whenever you want it.

Angrily shutting down and turning away. If you're dealing with frequent rejection, you'll likely feel angry and hurt. These feelings are natural, but if you punish your spouse by being passive-aggressive or outright hostile, you're slamming on the brakes. Instead of shutting down, learn how to talk about this subject. Get professional help if you need it. It isn't acceptable for your spouse to unilaterally decide your marriage will have little to no sex, nor is it okay to demand it and punish your spouse if you aren't getting it. You have to learn how to negotiate.

Personalizing the rejection. I hear things like "I shouldn't have to beg for sex" or "I don't want sex if my spouse doesn't want me." But your spouse's lack of desire might have nothing to do with you and everything to do with him or her. In marriage, we need to learn to ask for what we want, deal with the disappointment of not getting it, and do the work of negotiating a healthy solution for both partners.

Accepting a low-sex marriage with defeat. If your spouse wants sex less often than you do (or not at all) and you don't force it, what are your options? Get help! Don't settle for a sexless marriage; the resentment that might build could destroy your relationship.

If you're the "*lower-desire*" *spouse*, it's important for you to acknowledge your spouse's disappointment and frustration and to try to find a solution to the problem as a team. Common traps for the lower-desire spouse include the following:

Minimizing your spouse's frustration. I've heard phrases like "All he wants is sex" or "Nothing can satisfy her." I once heard a wife say she didn't care if her husband had an affair if he would just leave her alone. She didn't mean it, but her words were devastating to her husband. When you have the lower desire, you have more power over your spouse than you might realize. Your spouse wants something only you can give, and this puts him or her in a vulnerable position.

Ignoring the problem. Not wanting sex is one thing, but deliberately denying your spouse sex is not biblical. If you're struggling with sexual desire, find out why. See a physician and/or therapist. It isn't wise or healthy simply not to have sex and make your partner deal with it alone. You may have valid reasons for not having sex, such as past trauma or a physical condition, but it is your responsibility to find the help you need to address this issue.

Avoiding your partner in order to avoid having sex. The first thing that usually disappears in a marriage in which one partner is avoiding sex is physical affection. You may be afraid to cuddle, hug, or share kisses because it could lead your partner to initiate sex. But this only contributes to the pain and rejection your partner feels and creates more distance between you. It can be helpful to create "no-sex zones" to alleviate this—times when you want to be close but not be pressured to have sex.

EXERCISE: DISCUSSING DESIRE

Answer the following questions, then discuss your answers with your spouse.

How often would you like to have sex each week?

If you are the higher-desire spouse, how are you dealing with it?

If you are the lower-desire spouse, how are you dealing with it?

Are you openly sharing your concerns and frustrations about your desire differences? If not, why?

What can your spouse do or say that would make it easier to discuss sex?

SEXUAL (MIS)COMMUNICATION

Write out Song of Solomon 7:7–8.

CASE STUDY: ERIC AND SHANNON

Eric and Shannon came to see me because they weren't having sex. Eric was the lower-desire spouse, and he avoided all situations in which Shannon might be open to initiating. Shannon was confused, hurt, and angry. "I'm the only woman I know whose husband isn't chasing her around the house wanting sex," she said. "What's wrong with me? What's wrong with him?" In the session, Eric seemed reserved and said he just wasn't interested in sex, but when I got him alone, he told me that once, early in their relationship, he'd had some performance issues during a sexual encounter. Shannon made what he interpreted as a "cutting remark" about his masculinity. When I got them back together again, Eric confessed to Shannon how hurt he was and how he became anxious it would happen again. His resentment grew over the years until he decided he would rather not have sex than deal with the anxiety and humiliation. Shannon was shocked. She remembered the situation very differently. She hadn't intended to hurt Eric; in fact, she'd thought she was making light of the event to minimize his embarrassment. She was sad to learn that this unintentional wound had been festering for years. Eric and Shannon had some work to do around communication and reviving a sex life that had dwindled, but they were able to do both successfully.

As you can see from these verses, the Bible is very frank and open about sex, and you'll be happier and more fulfilled if you follow suit. Many marital issues around sex happen because couples just don't talk about it. It's okay to be uncomfortable; stretch yourself to have the difficult conversations. Every day, I help couples talk to each other about what they like and don't like in the bedroom, and usually, it just takes a little push to get them over the initial embarrassment so that they can discuss it openly.

Here are some of the most common sexual-miscommunication issues I hear:

- One partner thinks sex is too boring or predictable and wants to spice it up but doesn't know how to say so.
- One thinks he or she is initiating sex but the other is missing the cues.
- One doesn't ever feel it's okay to say no, or says no in hurtful ways.

- One has sexual preferences but is too shy to ask for what he or she wants.
- One or both aren't very educated about the female orgasm, so it isn't happening very often.
- One or both have unrealistic expectations about what sex "should" be.
- One partner just wants their spouse to "want them" and feels talking about or negotiating sex is a turnoff.

EXERCISE: HAVE THE CONVERSATION

List some things that you love about the way you and your spouse have sex. What specific activities do you enjoy and why?

_____

_____

_____

Is there anything your spouse is doing during sex that you would like him or her to stop doing?

_____

_____

_____

Is there any aspect of your sexual relationship where you feel insecure, uncertain, or timid?

Do you feel confident in your lovemaking skills? If not, why not?

Is there anything you would like your spouse to show you or teach you in regard to pleasing them sexually? What specifically would you like to know?

Is there anything you want your spouse to know about your sexual preferences?

How would you like your spouse to initiate sex and when?

If you initiate and your spouse isn't interested, how would you like him or her to decline? Write out specific phrases for your partner to use.

Is there any aspect of your sexual relationship you want to discuss that isn't mentioned here?

REVIEW

Here's a quick review of what we learned in this chapter:

- Sexual desire differences are a common occurrence in marriage. It is helpful to know what accelerates your desires and what puts on the brakes.
- Sex is never dirty or shameful in the confines of marriage between two consenting adults.
- Sexual trauma can affect the way you view and experience sex today, but it isn't your shame to carry. Be proactive in getting the help you need to heal if sexual trauma is keeping you from experiencing God's beautiful gift of sex with your spouse.
- The Bible is open and frank about sex, and your marriage will benefit if you get comfortable talking about it, too. Learning to face the flinch of discomfort when talking about sex will create more intimacy and connection between you. It's okay to feel shy or awkward. Just do it!

TAKE COURAGE AND DO IT

Here are some actions to take this week to increase love, joy, and peace in your sexual relationship with your spouse:

1. Spend some time in prayer and ask God to reveal where you're holding back sexually with your spouse and why. If you feel your spouse is holding back, ask God to give you wisdom, guidance, and patience as you discern how to approach your spouse about the issue.
2. If there are aspects of sex that make you feel uncertain or inadequate, see the resources on page 150 for suggestions on books about sex and begin educating yourself.
3. If you're the lower-desire spouse, make the commitment to begin figuring out what you could do to activate your accelerator or deactivate your brakes.
4. If you have experienced sexual trauma or feel you need help navigating sexual discussions with your spouse, search for a Christian counselor in your local area.

COMMITMENT

God takes marriage very seriously. To understand God's view of commitment in marriage, you have to understand that marriage is a covenant, which is more than a simple promise—it's a binding agreement between two parties, with each other and with God. Covenants are not broken lightly. Sometimes divorce is a sad necessity, but most marriages can and should be saved. Most people recognize the value of long-lasting, mature love, but many are unsure of what that looks like or how to achieve it. This chapter will help you find love, joy, and peace in your marriage long into the future.

▷—♡→

MARRIAGE OVER TIME

In the beginning, relationships are usually intense, as the newness of it all brings great highs. This temporary phase typically lasts less than two years, but it's the main focus of Hollywood romances—and a breeding ground for unrealistic expectations. I see marriages end when the relationship moves out of this stage into the growth phase and couples think they've lost their feelings of love and connection. This is tragic, really, because as the relationship matures, passion returns, and couples report higher satisfaction in the later stages of marriage than during the infatuation phase. When a relationship matures, familiarity combines with grace and perspective to create a special union.

BEYOND INFATUATION

Write out John 15:12.

God loves us because of who *He* is, not because of who *we* are. We can rebel and act in unlovable ways, and still the Father loves us because He is faithful. God keeps His commitments. If you're going to love your spouse the way God loves you, your focus has to be on your commitment rather than your feelings or your spouse's behavior. This is a critical concept to grasp if you want to have a long-lasting marriage. It doesn't mean you should ignore your emotions or any marital problems. It means that being in love is a feeling, and like any other feeling, it comes and goes. You won't always *feel* sad or happy or angry or in love. But if your decision to be married is based on commitment, you'll show up and choose to love even when your feelings don't match your promises.

Think back to your early days together. What attracted you most about the person you married?

Can you pinpoint a moment of disillusionment when you realized this relationship may not have been what you expected? If so, what was the event?

How did you handle yourself during this time?

What do you miss most about your relationship from the first two years?

What do you think about the idea of love as a commitment rather than a feeling? Would you want your spouse to be focused on commitment over feelings? Why?

How would your attitude or behavior toward your spouse change if you chose to love even when you weren't feeling particularly "in love"?

Write out Ephesians 4:13-15.

Relationships evolve over time, even our relationships with God. People grow; dynamics change. Many couples miss the excitement and intense feelings of the early stage of their union and often come to therapy hoping to go back to those feelings. But, truly, that isn't possible or even healthy. Wishing to go backward is like trying to keep your children from growing up; it's impossible. Just as Ephesians describes, as you and your spouse live together and learn more about each other, you grow in fullness and knowledge. Coming together in unity takes time and can be quite painful as we struggle through differences. But if you persist through the struggle of growth, you'll reap joy and peace as you learn and build each other up in love.

The transition between infatuation and maturity can be so hard that one or both partners gives up. This in-between place can be long and lonely. Some couples get stuck here and cannot move forward without help. If you do find yourself here, it helps to remember your commitment until your feelings catch up again. Below are some of the signs that indicate that you or your spouse may be in this critical place of growth. Check all that apply.

- ☐ You consistently focus more on your spouse's flaws than on his or her strengths.

- ☐ You feel lonely and disconnected but can't share this with your spouse.

- ☐ One or both of you is frequently angry or irritated with the other. Fighting becomes more frequent.

- [ ] You'd rather talk to someone else about your thoughts and feelings than your spouse.
- [ ] You start to feel trapped or smothered and may fantasize about leaving the marriage.
- [ ] You withdraw emotionally and/or sexually from the relationship.
- [ ] You start to think that you love your spouse but aren't *in love* with him or her.
- [ ] You feel insecure about your spouse's love and affection and frequently ask for reassurance.
- [ ] You tiptoe around your spouse to avoid upsetting him or her.
- [ ] You and your spouse spend more time apart (at work, with individual friendships, on individual hobbies, etc.).
- [ ] You feel more like roommates than a married couple.

If you checked even one of these, congratulations! It means your marriage is maturing. Don't panic and don't give up. These feelings are normal. Finding yourself in a hard place does not mean your marriage is over or that you'll never have warm feelings of love and connection again. It does mean it's time to roll up your sleeves and get to work. Don't ignore the signs and hope things get better on their own. The sooner you deal with this, the easier it is to get unstuck. The first thing to do is talk with your spouse to get a better understanding of what's happening from both of your perspectives.

EXERCISE: ARE YOU IN A SEASON OF GROWTH?

Discuss with your spouse the signs listed above. Do any resonate with either of you? What are you feeling or seeing in yourself or your spouse that concerns you?

If you're in a long season of difficulty, what steps have you taken to improve your situation? Have you talked to a pastor, read books about marriage, or sought professional help?

What are some of the blessings you're experiencing as your relationship matures (for example, more confidence, more comfortable familiarity)?

What have you come to learn about your spouse as you grow in fullness and knowledge together that you didn't know when you first got married?

What are you willing to do to help move through some of these difficulties?

_____

_____

_____

_____

_____

START WORKING ON YOU

Write out Matthew 7:5.

_____

_____

_____

It's so easy to believe that your marriage would improve if your spouse could or would change. But focusing on the other person keeps you stuck. In fact, the main thing that prevents success in marriage counseling is when spouses focus more on their partners instead of acknowledging their own faults and areas for improvement.

It might seem counterintuitive, but if you keep the focus on yourself, you'll have a much better chance to improve your marriage. Every action creates a reaction. Your newfound focus, clarity, and positive attitude will influence your spouse's behavior.

Describe the marriage you want to enjoy with your partner. Try to be as specific as possible and stay away from vague ideas like "I want to be happy." You might write: "I want a marriage where my partner and I work out problems without big blowups," "I want us to have sex at least once a week," or "I want my spouse to ask me about my day."

What are some things *you* would need to change to bring you closer to the marriage you described, such as being less reactive, listening more intently, or initiating sex more often?

THE BENEFITS OF THERAPY

Marriage counseling is not just for couples on the brink of divorce. In fact, the sooner you deal with issues, the easier they are to resolve (and the less time and money you'll spend in therapy). A good therapist will give you a safe space to be heard and help you see how you're contributing to the issues in your marriage. Even scheduling an appointment can be helpful: It shows you're motivated to improve the situation and gives you both hope for a brighter future. Here are some tips on finding the right counselor:

Find a counselor who specializes in working with couples. Look for someone with a caseload minimum that is at least 75 percent couples work.

Make sure the counselor is pro-marriage. Many therapists are marriage neutral and may even encourage divorce. Choose one who values the institution of marriage.

Don't look for the cheapest option. Counseling can be expensive, but it's an investment. Expect to pay $125 to $300 an hour.

Give your counselor feedback. No counselor is at his or her best in every session. If things aren't going well or you don't feel like your therapist is helping, speak up. It's your investment and your responsibility to make sure you're getting what you need. Don't just stop going—instead, give your counselor a chance to make adjustments. This is a collaborative effort. It requires teamwork to get the best results.

What internal obstacles might get in the way of you making those changes (for example, "It's hard to manage my emotions," "I get defensive easily," "I don't like to ask for what I want")?

What are you willing to do to overcome your internal obstacles, such as get counseling, speak up and be more honest, or learn to self-regulate emotionally?

DOES GOD ALLOW DIVORCE?

Infidelity, addictions, and abuse are good reasons to question whether or not you want to stay in a marriage. Even so, believers are often confused about what God thinks about divorce. Although it's never encouraged or commanded, God does give provisions that allow for divorce in some situations.

Write out 1 Corinthians 7:15.

Write out Matthew 19:9.

_____

_____

God mentions infidelity and abandonment as reasons to divorce, but what about abuse in the marriage? Does God expect us to stay in abusive marriages? There is no scripture that specifically says we can or cannot divorce our spouses due to abuse, but if we compare our relationships with each other to our relationships with God, it makes sense that unrepentant, unchanging abuse would be a reason to terminate the marriage.

Write out 1 John 3:6.

_____

_____

Write out Hebrews 10:26-27.

_____

_____

The Bible says if we sin deliberately and repeatedly, we sever our relationship with God. Why would He hold us to our marital covenant under the same conditions? When we harden our hearts to God, we're willfully abandoning and betraying Him. An abusive spouse is deliberately and repeatedly disobeying the biblical command to love his or her spouse, and this disobedience is also a form of abandonment and betrayal.

EXERCISE: WILLFUL SINNING

Why do you think willful sin separates us from God?

What would you consider to be examples of willful sinning against the marriage covenant?

CHOOSING TO STAY FAITHFUL

Write out Psalm 100:5.

The Bible tells us that God will be faithful to us forever. Isn't it comforting to know that God has committed to an eternal relationship with you? You never have to worry that He'll toss you aside or decide He doesn't love you anymore. You can rest in the security of your relationship with Him. Marriage can only give security to the degree of your level of commitment. I want to know my husband is going to be there if I become sick or disabled. I want to know he'll choose to love me even on days I don't look or act my best. This requires both of us to commit to our marriage for as long as we both live. New love is sweet, but mature love is far more precious because it brings security and peace.

EXERCISE: WRITE NEW VOWS

If you're like most couples, your vows on your wedding day consisted of you agreeing to the minister's questions about loving, honoring, and cherishing your spouse. Take some time and think about your marriage and your level of commitment to stay faithful. Write new vows that reflect your understanding of God's design for the covenant of marriage. Find a quiet space where you can be alone. Light a candle and read your vows to each other and before God. Pray for God to bless your marriage, and seal your renewed commitment with a kiss.

CASE STUDY: PATRICE AND LESLIE

Patrice and Leslie have been married for more than 25 years. They have highs and lows, like every other couple, but they don't wait until the lows get critical before coming in. They understand that you don't wait until you get a cavity to go to the dentist—you go twice a year to make sure your teeth are healthy. They see me about twice a year for the same kind of preventive care, very intentionally checking in to make sure things stay healthy between them. They don't just want a so-so relationship. They come in wanting me to challenge them and find ways they can improve their relationship skills. They're both open to hearing feedback, and instead of getting defensive, they want to learn more. I love working with them because they're teachable and motivated. One of the first things I always ask this couple is "What are you *not* talking about?" That question has started some great conversations!

A BRIGHT FUTURE

Write out Jeremiah 29:11.

God keeps His past promises, but He is also very invested in our future. Likewise, a good marriage needs you to not only remember your commitment from the past but also plan for the future. When we share goals and dreams for the future with our spouses, we're deepening the joy and the bond of marriage. Shared visions give us hope and something to strive for together. Plus it's fun, and your marriage needs a hearty dose of playfulness and fun on a regular basis. Don't be afraid to dream big.

Make a marriage "bucket list." You might include things like homeownership, kids, travel, and desired career paths.

5 YEARS   **10 YEARS**   **15 YEARS**

Create a vision board illustrating your list. You could simply write a list or make a project of it, cutting pictures from magazines or making sketches.

Create a timeline of five-year intervals. If things work out as you hope, where would you place your bucket-list items?

20 YEARS   **25 YEARS**   **30 YEARS**

REVIEW

Here's a quick review of what we focused on in this chapter:

- Marriage is a covenant between spouses and with God. Covenants are more than promises and should be taken seriously.
- Relationships go through phases of growth and maturity that may be painful, but this usually doesn't mean the marriage needs to end.
- If you feel stuck in your marriage, start by changing your own bad habits or failings. You might be in what I call "the growth phase."
- God allows the covenant to be broken with divorce when there is betrayal or abandonment.
- Your marriage is only as secure as your level of commitment, which goes beyond your feelings.

TAKE COURAGE AND DO IT

Congratulations! You've reached the end of this workbook. I hope it's been a rewarding journey for both of you, and I pray God blesses your marriage richly as you continue to learn more about yourselves and each other. The following final exercises are designed to help you launch toward a future filled with love, joy, and peace.

1. Find a happily married couple who has been together longer than you and your spouse and ask them to mentor you and your spouse for the next year. This might work like a small group at church where you meet at least once a month. Use the time to talk about your marriage, study scripture, pray together, and receive wise, godly counsel.
2. Print out your new vows from page 144 on beautiful paper and frame them. Hang them where you'll see them often.
3. Commit to finding and attending one to two marriage retreats or conferences each year. Look online, register early, and put them on your calendar.

4. Consider renewing your vows each year on your anniversary. You can do this privately or invite close friends to witness them.
5. Start saving for one of your bucket list ideas. Each week, drop loose change into a jar or add regular amounts to a special account each month.
6. Start a savings account for future marriage counseling. Don't wait until there is a huge problem to get help. Consider finding a counselor you like and checking in with him or her once or twice a year as a sort of preventive care.

I leave you with a final blessing, borrowed from Paul's letter to the Philippians: "And this is my prayer: that your love may abound more and more in knowledge and depth of insight, so that you may be able to discern what is best and may be pure and blameless for the day of Christ, filled with the fruit of righteousness that comes through Jesus Christ—to the glory and praise of God" (Philippians 1:9–11).

RESOURCES

⊳—♡→

THE MARRIAGE PLACE

My practice helps couples navigate matters such as affairs, communication problems, intimacy issues, family struggles, and more. Even though The Marriage Place is located in the Dallas area, we work with people all over the world. Our marriage coaches are expertly trained to work with both couples and individuals, using video as a means to conduct sessions. For more information, contact us at www.themarriageplace.com.

BOOKS

- *How We Love: Discover Your Love Style, Enhance Your Marriage* by Milan and Kay Yerkovich
- *The Five Love Languages: The Secret to Love That Lasts* by Gary Chapman
- *The Five Languages of Apology: How to Experience Healing in All Your Relationships* by Gary Chapman and Jennifer Thomas
- *The New Rules of Marriage: What You Need to Know to Make Love Work* by Terrence Real
- *Financial Peace: Restoring Financial Hope to You and Your Family* by Dave and Sharon Ramsey
- *She Comes First: The Thinking Man's Guide to Pleasuring a Woman* by Ian Kerner
- *The Emotionally Destructive Marriage: How to Find Your Voice and Reclaim Your Hope* by Leslie Vernick

SUPPORT FOR VICTIMS OF DOMESTIC ABUSE

The National Domestic Violence Hotline
1-800-799-7233 (SAFE)
www.TheHotline.org
www.NCADV.org/get-help

National Center on Domestic Violence, Trauma & Mental Health
1-312-726-7020 ext. 2011
www.NationalCenterDVTraumaMH.org

National Resource Center on Domestic Violence
1-800-537-2238
www.NRCDV.org
www.VAWnet.org

REFERENCES

Bancroft, John, Cynthia A. Graham, Erick Janssen, and Stephanie A. Sanders. "The Dual Control Model: Current Status and Future Directions." *Journal of Sex Research* 46, no. 2-3 (2009): 121–42.

Barna Group. "New Marriage and Divorce Statistics Released." March 31, 2008. www.barna.com/research/new-marriage-and-divorce-statistics-released.

Bowen, Kim. "How Healthy Is Your Relationship?" The Marriage Place. 2017. www.themarriageplace.com/marriage-quiz-new.

De Cadanet, Amanda. "More Women Watch (and Enjoy) Porn Than You Ever Realized: A Marie Claire Study." October 19, 2015. www.marieclaire.com /sex-love/a16474/women-porn-habits-study.

Horymski, Chris. "How Much Does the Average American Have in Savings?" MagnifyMoney. Lending Tree, April 28, 2019. www.magnifymoney.com/blog /news/average-american-savings.

Kosloski, Philip. "3 Methods of Prayer That Will Change Your Life." February 2, 2015. www.philipkosloski.com/three-methods-of-prayer-that-will-change-your-life.

Magon, Navneet, and Sanjay Kalra. "The Orgasmic History of Oxytocin: Love, Lust, and Labor." *Indian Journal of Endocrinology and Metabolism.* Medknow Publications, September 15, 2011. www.ncbi.nlm.nih.gov/pmc/articles /PMC3183515.

Northwestern Mutual. "New Data: Personal Debt On The Rise Topping $38,000 Exclusive Of Mortgages." August 14, 2018. https://news.northwesternmutual .com/2018-08-14-New-Data-Personal-Debt-On-The-Rise-Topping-38-000 -Exclusive-Of-Mortgages.

RAINN. "Children and Teens: Statistics." Accessed July 16, 2019. www.rainn.org /statistics/children-and-teens.

Yaffe, Philip. "The 7% Rule: Fact, Fiction, Or Misunderstanding." Ubiquity. ACM, October 2011. ubiquity.acm.org/article.cfm?id=2043156.

Your Brain on Porn. "Relevant Research and Articles About the Studies." Accessed July 16, 2019. www.yourbrainonporn.com/relevant-research-and -articles-about-the-studies.

INDEX

⊳—♡→

A

Abuse, 5, 8, 70, 87, 89, 117, 141–142
Accelerators, sexual, 118–121
Apologizing, 62–63
Appreciation, 18, 75–76, 79
Areas of authority, 79–82
Avoiders, 53–54

B

Boundaries, 57, 89–91, 95
Brakes, sexual, 118–121
Budgeting, 105–108

C

Chapman, Gary, 18, 63
Charitable giving, 102
Code of conduct contract, 59
Commitment
  faithfulness, 143–144
  focusing on yourself, 138–141, 148
  to the future, 145–147
  love as a, 132–134
  transition from infatuation to maturity,
    135–138, 148
Communication
  about sex, 124–129
  with each other, 8–20
  elements of, 8, 21
  with God, 2–8
  healthy, 15–17, 21
  hurtful, 10–15, 21
  importance of, 1
  love languages, 18–20, 21

Compromising, 76–77, 82
Conflict
  avoider style of, 53–54
  benefits of healthy, 47–48, 66
  controller style of, 54
  de-escalation strategies, 57–60
  healthy, 44–47
  making repair, 62–65
  pleaser style of, 52–53
  professional help for, 67
  reconciliation, 60–62
  styles, 52–56, 66
  time-outs, 51
Connection
  awareness of disconnectors, 34–36, 40
  with each other, 31–40
  with God, 24–30
  importance of, 23
  inappropriate, 35
  rituals, 32–34, 40
Controllers, 54
Covenant, marriage as a, 131, 148

D

Date nights, 37, 41
Desire, 121–124, 129
Divorce, 141–143, 148
Dual control model (DCM) of sexual response,
  118–121

E

Emotional regulation, 10, 16–17
Emotions, managing during conflict, 45–47,
  49–52, 66

Empathy, 35
Employment, 100–101
Equality, 71–72

F

Faithfulness, 143–144
Family
   God as the perfect parent, 93–95
   in-laws, 92, 95
   of origin, 86, 95
   parents, 86–91, 95
Finances. *See Money*
Financial Peace (Ramsey), 109
Five Languages of Apology, The (Chapman
   and Thomas), 63
Five Love Languages, The (Chapman), 18
Forgiveness, 63–66

G

God
   communicating with, 2–8
   connecting with, 24–30
   faithfulness of, 144
   as the perfect parent, 93–95
Greatest Commandment, 24–28

I

In-laws, 92, 95
Intercessory prayer, 3
Intimacy. *See also Sex*
   importance of connection, 37
   physical, 33, 41
   through prayer, 6, 20

L

Lectio divina, 3
Listening, 8–9, 20
Love
   for abusive parents, 87
   as a commitment, 132–134

communicating with actions, 18–20, 21
Greatest Commandment, 24–28
and respect, 74–75, 82

M

Marriage counseling, 140
Marriage quiz, 38–40
Mistakes, acknowledging, 62
Money
   budgeting, 105–108
   giving, 102
   mistakes, 108–110
   saving, 103–105
   and values, 98–99, 110
   working, 100–101

N

Negotiation, 77–78, 82

P

Parents. *See also In-laws*
   honoring, 86–87, 95
   leaving and cleaving, 89–91, 95
   setting boundaries with, 91
Partnership
   areas of authority, 79–82
   compromising, 76–77, 82
   impasses, 78–79
   love and respect, 74–75, 82
   meaning of, 69
   negotiating, 77–78, 82
   submission and equality, 70–74, 82
Pleasers, 52–53
Pornography, 120
Prayer and praying
   as a couple, 5–8
   methods of, 2–3
   through scripture, 3–4

R

Reconciliation, 60–65, 66, 87
Respect, 74–75, 82

S

Servant leadership, 70
Sex
    frequency of, 117–121
    miscommunication about, 124–129
    mismatched drives, 121–124, 129
    purpose of, 114
    and shame, 114–116
    and trauma, 117, 129
Sin, 142–143
Spiritual discipline, 29–30, 40
Stewardship, 103–105
Submission, 70–74, 82

T

Therapy, 140
Thomas, Jennifer, 63
Time-outs, 51
Tithing, 102
Trauma, sexual, 117, 129
Trinity, 71–72

V

Vows, 144

W

Wages, 100–101
Walking prayer, 3
Working, 100–101

ACKNOWLEDGMENTS

▷—♡→

This book could never have been written without the love and support of my husband, John. We are still married today because of your faithful perseverance and obedience to God. Thank you for your enduring commitment when things got really hard. You have always been my safe place. I love you and the life we have built together.

Thank you to my sons, Thomas and Alex, for all your support and cheerleading. You guys are the absolute best! If you follow your dad's lead, you'll be amazing husbands and fathers one day. My prayer is that you will find someone who loves God more than she loves you and that together you will work hard to build strong, healthy marriages.

Mom and Dad, growing up in your home, I got a front-row view of your marriage and witnessed many of the highs and lows. Thank you for never giving up on your covenant marriage. You've stuck it out for over 50 years now, and I'm so grateful for your commitment and the legacy you are leaving. I love you both.

Sara Snyder, thank you for your spiritual mentorship and friendship over the past two decades. You taught me how to receive God's love, and that has made all the difference. I'm fairly certain it saved my life. Sweet, precious friend, I love you BIG.

ABOUT THE AUTHOR

▷—♡→

Kim Bowen is a licensed professional counselor who founded The Marriage Place in 2013. She frequently writes blogs and newsletters that have been featured in various publications. She has been married to her husband, John, for more than twenty-nine years. They reside in Allen, Texas, and are currently enjoying their newly empty nest.